GETTING

COMFY

YOUR MORNING GUIDE TO DAILY HAPPINESS

JORDAN GROSS

YOUR FREE BONUS GIFT!

As part of my gratitude to my readers for purchasing this book, I'm giving away:

A Free Gift!

Your gift is an actual Getting COMFY routine for an entire week that I have used in the past. It is a phenomenal way to get started and kick-start your journey!

Find it here: http://getting-comfy.com/

TABLE OF CONTENTS

57% of Americans are snoozers, 76% wake up abruptly, and only 33% define their waking up experience as "good".

More than 41 million Americans experience some type of mental illness in any given year, according to the Substance Abuse and Mental Health Services Administration, a branch of the US Department of Health and Human Services in Washington, D.C., up 16% since 2000.

Millennials in particular are the most overstressed generation, with 1 in 5 experiencing some sort of depression, anxiety or mental illness.

THIS IS NOT A BOOK rooted in science or statistics. And those are all of the numbers, percentages, and factoids you are going to see for the remainder of our time together. Rather, Getting COMFY is based on experimentation, making myself a human lab rat every single morning, pushing my body, trying new experiences, and instilling the confidence in myself to pursue these new experiences and share with you the ones that work. In a society based on constant external pressures to succeed, Getting COMFY is an internal method that thwarts these pressures, especially for a millennial, right when we wake up. It is a 5-step voyage that soothes the mind and energizes the body as you approach the rest of the day. We may have un-COMFY feelings with our bodies, our jobs, or our schoolwork. This has happened to me too. But the way we respond to these situations is what we can control, and what ultimately leads us to become the people we strive to be.

I was slightly overweight growing up. Ok fine, I was fat, quite fat. Years ago, I remember having this amazing waiter while eating lunch with my friend and his family. He cracked jokes with us, gave us free samples, and developed a genuine bond with our table. Toward the end of the meal, as the conversation got more personal, he mentioned that my friend and his sisters must be related, and I was not part of the family. A curious child, I asked why and how he knew that, and with mild to no hesitation he replied,

"Well, them 3 are skinny."

This was a long time ago, and maybe he wasn't even trying to be mean, just honest. But this hurt me. This phrase still rings in my ears. It was the first time I felt uncomfortable in my own skin, with my appearance, with the direction of my life. Even at age 10, I noticed more things about me that I did not like. I pushed the boundaries of the trifecta and demonstrated the quadfecta—I was heavy, I had long hair and was commonly mistaken for a girl, I had glasses because I was cross-eyed, and not to mention, my last name is Gross, so I already had people saying, "ew" from just hearing my name and not even having yet seen me!

All I wanted to do was stay in my bed, in my room, and never come out. Every time I awoke from a dream feeling happy and confident, I cringed at the thought that I would have to face my peers, hear my last name be called on the attendance sheet, take my shirt off to go in the pool. I didn't fully understand what I was doing at the time, but

I needed to do something, and that something truly changed my life. So instead of sleeping all the time and hiding these fears, withdrawing and playing video games, I did the opposite. I began waking up just a little bit earlier each day and started moving around the house. I jogged in the shower, ran up and down the stairs, stood to watch TV instead of sat. I worked harder on my sports teams. Little by little, my body changed and so did my mentality. I kept the long hair until college and eventually got rid of the glasses, but as my body morphed into something I was proud of, I became COMFY with my appearance, my mentality, my name, and all other elements of life.

This is not a book about weight loss. It is not a book about feeling ugly, disliked, or unusual. It is a book about a certain mindset. The mindset to make a change, to do something different, to assess exactly what it is that is holding you back, and to turn these seemingly un-COMFY characteristics and experiences into ones in which you can Get COMFY. And what better time to start practicing that mindset than in the morning?

Morning routines are commonplace, saturated even. But there is no one morning routine that suits every person, which is why Getting COMFY is a collection of recommendations that emphasizes trial and error, provides actionable steps for you to take as you read, so that you know when a routine has become right for you.

Below is a brief breakdown:

C – Calm

"Down to the left, down to the right, down to the middle." I have had the same stretching routine since I joined my first travel soccer team when I was 8 years old. Stretching is such a relaxing activity that puts the mind and body at ease. Stretching, along with a variety of other soothing activities, halts that startled feeling we have when we wake up, and puts us in a positive, less anxious state of mind. C stands for Calm.

O – Openness

"You're not going to get good at golf until you get out and experience the course." This was career advice given to me about whether or not I should enter into the restaurant industry as my first job, or wait and try something else before pursuing my true aspirations. Without this conversation, and had I not reached out to somebody for advice, I would be going through the motions, longing to know what it would be like in a career that was desirable to me, rather than one I believed was desirable to others. It is essential that we are honest with ourselves and with others. O stands for Openness.

M – Movement

Since that day in the restaurant with my friends' family and that waiter, exercise has been my means of expression. To celebrate positive and blow off negative, exercise provides the release necessary to literally move forward past any situation. M stands for Movement.

F – Funny

As we pulled up to the crowded Walk for Multiple Sclerosis parking lot, my brother suggested, "Maybe if you tell them that mom has MS, they'll give us a great spot!" In our media driven, tragedy focused world, it is imperative that we find time to laugh. Using humor to overcome hardship, focusing on smiling right when we wake up rather than engulfing ourselves with the horrors of society is paramount. F stands for Funny.

Y – YOU

Understand yourself. Know yourself. Guide yourself. Take time every morning to practice something that brings joy to your life. Something that no matter what the rest of the day has in store, makes you feel accomplished, meaningful. My passion has been writing *Getting COMFY*. But it is your mission to understand what gets you giddy, what gets you excited, what makes you feel like a kid again. That is when you know you have passion. Y stands for YOU.

My father is a collection attorney. He is the nicest collection attorney you've ever met in your life, first of all, and second of all, he is one of the nicest all around people you've ever met in your life. But the description of a collection attorney runs counter to my father's personality. He essentially gets debtors to pay the money to the people whom they owe. I picture him as one of those tough guys who show up at your door and shake you around a little bit before you pay up, but in actuality, he is not that, not at all.

I never really cared and, in retrospect, selfishly never knew what he did because from the second I could spell law, my dad told me that I should choose my own career path and not be compelled to follow his. I learned what collecting was and characterized it as a legal bookie, claiming money owed from irresponsible gamblers. Not my dad, no way. But he is good at it, so he has been able to somewhat separate his work and home personalities in order to optimally perform in his career. To me, he is still that nice attorney who shows compassion when warranted. He and I know that there are billions of people in this world and some out there have it worse than others. So he takes into account one's personal and economic situation before collecting payment. It is what I consider an incredible sense of perspective that I aim for you to take away from this book.

It is cliché, but before Getting COMFY I felt like I had no direction. I was at a crossroads of banality and adventure that I believe many of us face as millennials entering the workforce or going to college and picking a major: do I work tirelessly to find a career that "fosters a collaborative learning environment and builds the skills necessary to progress onward in my field", or do I reject that fluffy BS and find something I want to do NOW that will be new, challenging, dangerous, and an escape from the safety of my peers? I chose the latter.

I made this decision because I started to Get COMFY. When I learned that my dad had to walk through the front door every single day and sort of flip a switch from work to home personality, I decided I was not going to put myself in a position where I could not be me all the time. I was going to discover what I loved through observation and execution, contemplation and discussion, experience and analysis. My "work-life balance" would not really exist because my goal is to remain the same person, have the same outlook and emotions in both work and life, and remain COMFY even in the most un-COMFY of environments.

My brother has also had a major impact on my Getting COMFY journey. Four years older than me, I looked to him for guidance, following his ideas and recommendations. Always a bit smarter than me in school, he went to Duke and studied Biology and Chemistry, dreaming of going to med school. He did not end up going to med school coming out of undergrad, but now 4 years later, he has retaken and dominated the MCAT, has experience in the healthcare consulting space, and is ready to revisit his original ambition of becoming Dr. Adam Gross.

This is the type of perseverance and triumph over setbacks that motivate me. This is the way we must all handle adversity. This is what the Getting COMFY mentality encapsulates.

And my mom? One of my greatest inspirations, don't worry, we will get to her soon enough. For now, let's understand a little bit more why you should listen to me, and take a chance on the advice I have for how to enhance your positivity and happiness in the morning and beyond.

You talkin' to me?
You talkin' to me?
YOU talkin' to ME?
Robert DeNiro, Taxi Driver

WHY ME?

"As I applied this magical gel, I created whimsical designs. I started off as Santa, and then moved on to a cowboy with a handlebar moustache. It was fresh, exciting, and new. My face is now a tattered war zone, a pawn in the chess board of personal hygiene."

I began writing *Getting COMFY* as a senior in college with little creative writing experience since my freshman year in high school. I wrote the short piece above about how my first time shaving was this monumental experience in my life that has now become a mundane part of my weekly routine, the theme of which I actually borrowed from one of my brother's college application essays. But I enjoyed writing it; I remember the smile on my face as I progressed from the first to the fifth page. Unfortunately, that is the most significant literary accomplishment I have in my life at this point, so I would understand if you decided to close this book and return it to the closest virtual bookstore (how do returns with online shopping work anyway?). But please don't! I urge you to give me a chance, because in this book I am solely trying to help you, and provide insight on how to live a happier, more optimistic lifestyle.

Why should you listen to me? Who am I and why do I think I know how to live life? The answers to these questions are quite important because frankly, you don't have to listen to anyone. Most learning about oneself comes from experiencing what you *don't* want to do, so at the minimum this book should allow you to assess your life and make a judgment as to what are the right methods for you.

Our data-overloaded world provides access to unlimited information, resulting in unlimited choices. As a result, you can combine the theories and options in this book with other articles and stories you have read to create personal life practices that fulfill your needs. These are guidelines, not demands. So at the end of the day, my goal is for *you* to pick and choose what is going to make *you* better, because we are not the same. I know and have evaluated what makes me happy and am putting it in general yet somewhat specific terms; but I cannot determine for you whether or not an activity I do will give you that "kid again" feeling that I get.

The first time we locked eyes was the first time I understood what it meant to hear the Beatles. She was a stunning display of perfect proportion, dressed marvelously but with a simple elegance, a smell so sweet you could not resist. She sat there and didn't say a word, but we both knew it was on me to take the initiative. Equipped with unrelenting confidence and experience in the field, I approached this delicacy and never looked back. This was my first encounter with Pizzeria Uno's Deep Dish Cookie Pizza.

What did you think I was talking about?!?!?!

As I gazed at that sizzling skillet and my fork effortlessly seeped into the center of this practically uncooked cookie, I knew it was a match made in heaven. Approaching just a few bites more, my parents took away the cookie, probably due to the thousands of calories and grams of sugar I had consumed. As a chubby little boy, I burst into tears.

My family and I have coined the term "cry dish" when we go to a restaurant. My palate has become more sophisticated since I met my first love at Pizzeria Uno, but our definition of cry dishes has not. A "crier" is a course of a meal that is so good that you want to start crying when you finish it. That last bite marks the end of a saga—an emulsion of flavors so beautiful that it actually brings you to tears. You seldom get a cry dish, but when you do, it hits you like a 100 mph fastball.

Cry dishes do not have to solely apply to meals. You can have cry vacations, cry dates, cry jobs, cry books. Criers are activities and items that you have enjoyed so much that you never want them to end. They have taken you on a path so memorable, that the only thing you can do as it ends is weep. Getting COMFY is a cry morning routine. I ensure you that every morning, just as you are about to finish up, you will either want to start over, or will be thinking about it all day until you can wake up and do it again. This daily 5-step journey will activate your body, clear your mind, and ensure an optimistic approach to your day. So let's Get COMFY, let's rejoice that our transformation together is about to commence, and let's start our cry routine.

Much of the motivation for Getting COMFY comes from when I started to listen to podcasts, mainly focused on personal development and how to live a more meaningful life. Instead of listening to music all the time at the gym or on a run, I started listening to an hour-long podcast and the time flew. As an uninvolved music listener who mainly knows only the top radio hits, I got tired of listening to the same songs on repeat. I'm also technologically challenged and have to wait for my friends to put music on my phone, so I figured it would be more effective to actively listen to things I wanted, rather than passively listen to my friends' music on a loop.

I also recently discovered an incredible style of living that the Danish call Hygge. Having not known about it before writing any of this, I was elated to see that there were similar views on life out there. Hygge is a psychological, social, or physical state in which all of one's needs are in balance. The philosophy of hygge is very similar to the philosophy of Getting COMFY. This methodology urges you to surround yourself with comfortable objects in your house, light a candle at dinner, or spend time with friends—small, simple actions that aim to improve your spirit.

This type of behavior is exactly what I want to encourage with Getting COMFY. These recommendations are not painstaking life changes that one must gradually implement and monitor over time. Rather, they are simplistic actions that will not disrupt one's day-to-day activities, but through their constant practice, will become completely life altering.

A few years ago my dad and I went to a burger place on Long Island, Bobby Flay's Burger Palace. Besides the fact that they had unbelievable burgers and shakes, they had a little twist on their burgers in which you could "crunchify" them by putting potato chips inside the sandwich. My dad was distraught. He had been putting potato chips in sandwiches for as long as I could remember. "I could have been Bobby Flay! He stole my idea!" my dad joked.

The thing about crunchifying, Hygge, or about an app like Instagram or Snapchat is that they are so simple and a million people have thought of the idea, or were even doing the idea before it was publicized. That's how I want you as a reader to feel about the advice in this book. Simplicity alone is not successful. But simplicity with proper implementation, this can be life changing.

I consider Getting COMFY an "IDUH" instead of an "idea" because it is something so simple to comprehend. It's something you will read or see and say, "duh", I can *do* that, I can *try* that, or even,

I have *done* that. Something like this provides the confidence to make a change and try something new right now, rather than presents a grandiose scheme that may take years of studying and analyzing to test. The changes and activities I am urging you to follow with your morning routine are not groundbreaking and there are not necessarily years of scientific research behind them. Rather, they are implementable strategies that are so easy to follow, yet so often overlooked or forgotten. But once they are ingrained in your mind and in your morning ritual, I promise you will feel and perform better in every aspect of life.

After listening to hundreds of hours of podcasts, I came across an interview with Hal Elrod—a wonderful speaker, life coach, entrepreneur, salesman, husband, father, you name it—and was immediately in awe of his wisdom. Hal is the author of *The Miracle Morning: The Not-So-Obvious Secret Guaranteed to Transform Your Life (Before 8AM)*, which has sold hundreds of thousands of copies, and is the benchmark for morning routine rituals. Essentially, I have listened to and read Hal's methods in detail, and put my own personal spin on them, which is exactly what I want you to do with my recommendations.

I've always had thoughts about writing a book, but between sports and academics in high school, and academics, social life, and extracurricular activities in college, I believed I didn't have the time to write something. That mentality changed the second I started waking up earlier.

It is difficult to fathom how almost everybody I know starting with friends just one year older than me have advised me to cherish the "freedom" I still have now, because it will only get worse from here on. But why does that have to be? Why can't I start to make my life better for myself, have more time to do what I love, and then express how I do this with all of you? I'm writing this book to tell you all that you can live the life you want even with that corporate 9 to whenever job, even as a student in middle school, high school or college, even as a parent, and even as a grandparent or great grandparent.

"It took X event for me to create Y result." There it is. The realization that a second in time, the "ahah" moment, the light bulb effect, the IDUH, whatever you want to call it, was necessary for somebody to take control of her or his life and create something meaningful. In my studying of the most successful people in the world, this is the formula for success. Many of them document a specific turning point in their lives when things finally started to click, pessimism turned to hope, ideas turned to pursuits. Oftentimes tragedy had to strike for them to realize you only get one life (sorry, but I will not write YOLO in a serious sentence, I will not do it), and they needed to start crafting it the way that they wanted, rather than allowing life to lead them. But I figure, why wait for the perfect timing, or the perfect alignment of the stars to start sharing best practices with other people and inspire them? I am in the midst of my Getting COMFY journey—writing this book and adapting to new endeavors—I practice this 5-step ritual to dissolve the pressures associated with these life events, and my aim for you is to work alongside your tour guide, rather than follow him.

I went to an excellent school, and I did pretty well. I attribute my academic success to time management, knowing my strengths, and using these strengths to give me an advantage in the classroom. You are smarter than I am. You are more mature than I am. You have the opportunity to become much more successful than I am. I can barely tie a knot, my dad pre-ties all my ties, and I'm pretty sure I forgot how to ride a bike if that is even possible. I haven't studied math or science since freshman year, I struggled in my economics classes, but I thrived because my skills as a hard-working, organized and time efficient student were optimized by choosing classes that I knew I would succeed in after much research.

I have also developed relationships with my professors and coworkers beyond the classroom and office. At the end of the day, they are still people, and while you are constantly evaluated on your knowledge of a particular subject at work or in school, a person is going to have a much harder time giving a bad grade or firing somebody they know and like over somebody who merely goes through the motions. There is no top-secret formula for maintaining a high GPA, getting a management position, or enjoying a high quality of life, but rather, it is learning enough about yourself to know what actions you must take in order to make you happy and provide the greatness you deserve.

As a millennial, I know that as we are more exposed to technology and information becomes so readily available, our attention spans are shrinking. We fail to focus on one thing for more than 2 minutes without looking away at our phones or computers. We can't read that paper, that report, that novel, or even fully enjoy a 30-minute show or movie because we are not invested in the material and would much rather be chatting with friends or looking online for things we want to see. In this book, I am trying to provide a release from the distractions and say, "read this if it truly interests you", because that is how you are going to get the most out of it. For these reasons, this book is going to:

1. Provide a variety of stories to grab your attention

2. Delve deep into my life and the lives of a few others to share how we have been impacted by the Getting COMFY mindset

3. Be short and to the point so you're not intimidated by a 300-page novel

4. Offer lists and examples of ideas and recommendations to implement into your routines, starting *now*

5. Create challenges for you to attempt and share with friends

The most important reason I want you to know about why I am writing this guide is that I genuinely feel it can help millions of people. I am not writing this because I want to begin a career as an author, because I want to gain praise among friends and family, or because I am looking to make money. This is a serious and meaningful representation of the methods I believe are most beneficial to living an optimistic, stress-free, and plain and simple, happy life. **Together, we are going to Get COMFY waking up in the morning, Get COMFY in un-COMFY situations, Get COMFY in our own skin, and Get COMFY with the way we live the rest of our lives.**

According to most studies, peoples number one fear is public speaking. Number two is death. Death is number two. Does that sound right? This means to the average person, if you go to a funeral, you're better off in the casket than doing the eulogy.
Jerry Seinfeld

WHY YOU SHOULD GET COMFY

You spend more time with yourself than anyone else in the world. So why wouldn't you invest in yourself and do things that constantly make you better, constantly make you happy, and constantly allow you to feel COMFY in your own skin every single day? It seems obvious right? By no means am I saying to be selfish and solely care about yourself, but rather I'm saying put time into what you know makes you the best version of you. **The more you invest in yourself, the more able you are to help those around you and succeed in what you really desire.**

Allow me to repeat . . . We spend more time with ourselves than anybody else in the world. So why not work on, polish, and Get COMFY with the person with whom we spend so much time? This is the critical message I want you to take from this book. If you don't learn anything else, I want you to learn that personal development is paradoxical—we must focus on ourselves because we are the most important people in our own lives—but in order to better ourselves we must better our relationships and we must learn from other people. The pinnacle of personal improvement comes from the openness toward and understanding of others, and our willingness to engage with others and incorporate their best strategies into our own lives. We must embrace developing ourselves because only then can we make the impact we desire for other people.

I have never regretted doing my COMFY routine. Instead of immediately telling you all of the amazing benefits of waking up early, I'd rather describe what happens when I skip the morning ritual.

A terrible ringing interrupts a pleasant dream, and I wake up startled. I get up, turn off the alarm, take a sip of water, go to the bathroom, walk back to my room, and think, what would another hour in bed really do? So I crawl back under the covers, and sleep for another hour. I wake up around 9, and have to be in class by 9:30; I rush to shower, throw clothes on, and run out the door. I don't even have time for food, let alone any sort of self-betterment in the few minutes I have between when I had to wake up and when I start my day. This is what most people will do—but it is not what I want to do, and more importantly, not what I want you to do.

I woke up on this day, at this particular time, because I *had* to, not because I *wanted* to, and this is the attitude most people have when they approach their day. How are we positioning ourselves for success if we think of starting the day as a chore, rather than embracing the day as a privilege? The answer is simple: we're not.

I won't lie to you, I have skip days—this is a work in progress for me just like it is you. I sometimes miss Getting COMFY because my own discipline is not fully there yet. On these days I am sluggish, the day feels rushed, it's more stressful, and I am filled with regret. What did that extra hour of sleep even do for me? What does it do for us? Nobody truly knows, so why not embark on activities in which we know the result, activities that will improve ourselves. All day I wonder how much better I

27

would be feeling if I had gone on that run, watched that video, or listened to that podcast. But let me tell you this: On days I do Get COMFY in the morning, I never feel this way. These days are filled with satisfaction, because whatever happens throughout, I know I had an unbelievable morning.

The Monday after the Kentucky Derby, I was feeling miserable when I woke up. I think we know why. I immediately went for the snooze button thinking God knows what as my eyes opened for the first time. I got an extra 47 minutes of sleep, and it did absolutely nothing. I felt as bad, if not worse than when I woke up, except now I was in a rush to get up and go. Feeling this way, I had no desire to interact with classmates, no desire to interact with professors, no desire to interact with anyone. Only the desire to curl up in a ball and get back into bed, which I certainly know will not do me any good in the long run.

No Snooze Challenge!

I have decided and realized that snoozing does not provide a positive experience to begin the day. There needs to be some incentive to prevent snoozing so I have developed a challenge, which I call the NO SNOOZE CHALLENGE. The challenge while simplistic is a refreshing way to start the day. Here it is:

1. Choose something you love and do almost everyday (watching TV, going to the gym, reading, playing an instrument, riding your bike)

2. Wake up in the morning

    a. Don't snooze!

    b. Snooze

3. If you go with option a, then you win!

4. If you go with option b and snooze, then for however long you snooze, you must take that amount of time away from the activity that you love on that particular day i.e. 15 minutes of snoozing = 15 minutes less watching TV.

This raises an interesting point though: what if you seriously feel like shit when you get up? This has certainly happened, and I am working on what to do. We haven't yet discussed our specific morning activities in detail, but most of them you can still do from the COMFY-ness of your own bed! So maybe you will skip your exercise, but you will still complete almost a full COMFY routine, which is

500x better than going back to sleep and doing nothing. You're giving your body time to slowly adjust, rather than keeping it in its sleep state, which helps improve how you function the remainder of the day.

There are also days in which you wake up and know you're feeling fully energized. When I was 8 years old, I played in the earliest soccer game of my life. It was a 7am Championship game of an indoor league, right in the heart of winter. To my parents, this must have been dreadful, waking up at 6 on a Saturday to go watch a bunch of 8-year olds chase a ball and hope that at some point one of them kicks it in the goal. But for me, it was the most exciting day of my life. I woke up naturally at 5 something, jumped out of bed, ran into my parents room and started singing "We are the Champions" until my parents joined me (pretty cocky at age 8, but we did end up winning). My happiness and excitement for the day brought a sense of delight to my parents that gave them this same sort of urgency to get up and enjoy their morning. **A major part of enjoying every morning is to reach inside for the kid in you and not be afraid to outwardly portray your excitement for the day ahead.**

The rest of this section will describe what to do to ensure a good night's sleep, so that you wake up pumped and thrilled to face the day. This whole Getting COMFY mentality may sound silly to you, but that is the point—it is a routine meant to bring lightheartedness to the start of your day—something to get you in the mindset that views life as a day at a time journey filled with inexplicable circumstances, but circumstances that can always be understood by working on yourself and what you love every morning.

These initial tips are not all my own. I have seen some of them in articles, read them in Hal Elrod's book, and heard them during podcasts or conversations with friends. They're almost so obvious that you may even be doing them from time to time, but the key is to do them all the time so that they become a trigger to your mind and body that it is time to enjoy the start of your day.

Let me take a step back and quickly talk about the night before. Contrary to what you may think, I love sleep. Sleep is glorious. You should get as COMFY and cozy in bed at night and have the best sleep of your life, but when that alarm goes off, it's time to have the best day of your life. This is a morning routine book, so I don't want to overload you with recommendations for the night before, but I will say one thing: Go to bed smiling, wake up happy. **Go to bed smiling, wake up happy.**

I don't literally mean lay in bed with a grin on your face until you fall asleep, but rather, ensure that you have some sort of happiness, laughter, or satisfaction right before you call it lights out. Never go to bed angry with somebody, in an argument, or after watching or reading something depressing, because then there is no excitement in your sleep, but rather contemplation. This contemplation does not carry over to the excitement you want to wake up with the next morning. Below are a few recommendations for what you can do right before bed:

1. **Watch a 15–30 minute TV episode, comedy special, or video** – I know that studies show it is detrimental to watch a screen before bed so watching TV, looking at your computer, or even reading your Kindle is frowned upon by most. However, that's not true for everyone. Watching these shows serves as a perfect close to the end of an amazing day. It's fitting to get under the covers, let your mind wander as you watch something you enjoy, and slowly drift into a phenomenal sleep.

2. **Write about today or tomorrow** – If you're a planner, this is perfect for you! It's a relatively painless process, which includes jotting a few things down that you want to get accomplished tomorrow. Or, if you'd rather reflect, write down a few things that you achieved that day. Think about all the positive things you were able to finish in such a short amount of time! Don't focus on what you have not yet done or what you forgot, but rather what you wanted to do and did, or what you want to do and will complete tomorrow.

3. **Talk to Mom!** – Everyone who knows me will tell you that I have a very close relationship with my mom, Linda. She's the type of Jewish mother that everybody wants and needs, so I make sure to call her every single day because I know that is what makes her happy, what makes her have the day that she desires. We talk for 5 minutes to an hour depending on the day, and it is a time for me to speak openly and freely (I know my mom is never judging me, so I can tell her whatever I want, without filter). It's the exact same as writing about what I did today, or what I

am going to do tomorrow, except I enjoy it more because I am receiving feedback from the other end. This does not only have to be mom! You can talk to dad (Hey Paul!), brothers (Hey Ad!) sisters, aunts, uncles, grandparents, anybody that will actively listen and provide you with an appropriate outlet to review your day and what is to come.

4. **Read** – Read a book! I used to hate reading and even ridiculed people that enjoyed it. Nerds! But I love being a reading nerd now. I love geeking out with people about what is in their library, or what books they love to share with others. Plus it takes a serious toll on my eyes and allows me to ease into an amazing sleep!

All of these recommendations enable you to fall asleep with a smile on your face, and in a state of peace, exactly what we want as we approach the unbelievably COMFY morning we have awaiting us. We are now all set to get up, get ready, and Get COMFY!

And for those who need that extra push to conquer the alarm clock, do this as soon as it starts ringing:

1. Eyes Open

2. FEET ON THE FLOOR

3. Splash cold water in your face

We'll get more into these as we move along, but for now we are about to embark upon our first morning practice. Remember not to stress about being perfect at this or seeing immediate results. Try to enjoy the process rather than get caught up with the result. Drumroll please . . .

Sit back, RELAX, and enjoy.
Every voiceover announcer ever

C - CALM

School, jobs, spouses, children, parents, bills, mortgages—we have a lot to think about everyday and it can get overwhelming. We are all startled by our alarm clocks and promptly begin thinking about the complex tasks we have ahead of us. We must find a way to rid ourselves of this instant worry.

Think about what the number one piece of advice is before somebody has a job interview, is about to star in a performance, is about to take a big test, or is about to step up to the plate. RELAX, calm your nerves, take deep breaths, and do not think too much. We are told to relax before movies, plays, and concerts because that is how we are going to maximize our enjoyment. This is the logic we should use to approach our day, and is the method we should practice to start it. If we go in anxious, with too much pressure on ourselves, we are going to be overcome by our own expectations of the end result, rather than focusing on the enjoyable ride it takes to get there.

I am not going to force any one practice on you that will without a doubt allow you to immediately get calm when you wake up. Rather, I will give you my own personal stories and provide recommend-dations that have worked for me, may not have worked, and some that work for others. Finding and toying with various forms of this routine is part of the fun in Getting COMFY.

Meditation

Oftentimes we say to save the best for last. But here I want to start with meditation, which could be the single best practice for calming your mind and body. But it is also the most complex and will take the longest to master.

I confess to you, I am not an expert at meditating. I don't enjoy being bad at anything, but many times I attempt to meditate, and I feel like I am not improving at all. But I keep practicing because I don't like to quit, and to an extent, it does calm me down.

What often happens is: I wake up, put my feet on the floor, drink water, go to the bathroom, come back, sit by my bed, and set my alarm for 5 minutes. Good start. But, the overwhelming majority of the time, I feel as if I fall back asleep for 5 minutes, which is obviously not the purpose at all!

But, those few times when something clicks, I open my eyes after 5 minutes, and my mindset is completely altered from anxious, wanting to jump back in bed, to excited and eager to begin the day.

There is so much research about meditation online and how to succeed in practicing it. A few non-pro tips from me would be to really focus on your breathing and to try your hardest not to let your mind wander—this is when the stress kicks in. So focus on a noise, focus on a particular sound, or repeat a "mantra". I won't delve into the spiritual research behind meditation (there are tons of resources out there for that), but I am asking you to trust me in that if you trust the process, you will see shockingly positive results and feel much more relaxed from the pressures that may arise in your life.

Another tip from my own experience is don't get back into bed to do this! I know there is a glaring juxtaposition here in that we want to Get COMFY in the morning during this process, but getting back into your bed is not the right answer for that! Sit on your floor, the couch, a chair, but don't lie down!

So many people use meditation as a means of success. Ross Goldberg is a Northwestern graduate with a very successful consulting career at Alvarez & Marsal. I was fortunate enough to get to know Ross at school, and with his easygoing, mild-mannered demeanor, I was not at all surprised to find out he practiced meditation.

I challenged myself as one of my 2016 New Year's Resolutions to meditate once per week after reading about all the physical, mental, and emotional benefits, as well as the positive impact it had on prominent businesspeople, athletes, and other social figures.

When I first started, I read articles, listened to podcasts/guided meditations, and read the book Zen Mind, Beginner's Mind, which Steve Jobs touted as having a huge influence on his career, in order to find what worked best for me personally. Ultimately, I found my sweet spot to be short (5-10 minute) guided meditations, primarily using the app Headspace.

I did achieve my resolution in 2016, and while I don't meditate once per week anymore, I still find it to be an effective way to "unplug" (understanding the irony in unplugging while still using an iPhone app to meditate) every few weeks. Juggling professional, social, and personal commitments in an "always on" culture, it's tough to slow down and really think about absolutely nothing for a while, but when I do find the time to meditate, I generally fall asleep more easily, wake up more clear-headed, and find myself noticeably sharper and more energized the next day.

I am extremely grateful for these comments from Ross. They even motivated me to start using Headspace, which is a fantastic way to practice meditation, especially for beginners. Ross affirms how calm it makes him, "unplugging" from a constantly plugged in society; something I can imagine is quite beneficial in the life of a consultant. He also mentions that many of the most influential and inspirational people in the world use meditation, so as an inspirational person himself, Ross knew and thankfully was able to experience the benefits of guided meditation.

I'm a big believer in focusing on my strengths and being aware of my weaknesses. But although meditation is not yet a particular strength of mine,

I still work at it because I know it will help in my personal development in the long term, and I know that personal development is the key to being comfortable with my life and achieving what I ultimately want to accomplish. Additionally, focusing on strengths and being aware of weaknesses is more advice for hard skills and not character traits. I can't hire anybody to meditate for me, so I have to get better at it on my own. At the same time, I realize that if something isn't working optimally, there must be another solution, so here are a few more recommendations for how you can calm down when you wake up.

Yoga

Spirituality is great, but I'm not the most spiritual of people, so it speaks volumes that I am a major proponent of two highly spiritual techniques to begin my day. Yoga is another fantastic activity that calms both the mind and the body. It ensures the clarity and serenity we need to combat our over-scheduled lives.

However, this one is also not my strong suit. I'm the guy in the back of a yoga class giggling when I'm told to close my eyes and rest in child's pose or get into downward dog. But, I have such a profound respect for the people that yoga hits on a deeper level. I appreciate people who are better than me at things—we should all treat people with the notion that they are better or smarter than us at something, and we should learn from that person.

I watch yogis practice their craft, and I am absolutely fascinated by the state of tranquility and satisfaction it brings to them. Their minds are completely at ease, they're so present, and they're truly living in the moment. This is exactly what we need if we are going to become more comfortable in every situation we face.

Stretching

We are now at my go-to activity. Stretching feels amazing. We used to stretch in gym class, on our youth sports teams, and we hated it then. But think about this—Our bodies felt pretty damn good right? Why don't we stretch anymore? Because we're not on teams? Because we have reached the shocking realization that we are no longer going to be professional athletes? No, it's because nobody is telling us to! I'm here to tell you to stretch for a few reasons. It's incredibly relaxing, it feels great, and your body will thank you for it. Also, if stretching is your first activity of the day, it will definitely help you get out of bed!

Stretching brings your body this exhilarating feeling that allows you to be loose for the rest of the day. You will start to feel positive about how good you feel, and that mind-body connection gives you exactly what you're looking for in personal development. Doesn't everybody stretch when they wake up anyway? You give a loud yawn and a big reach for the ceiling? Why not make it a real, beneficial routine?

A sample stretch routine to hit all the major areas of the body is a 20 count to all of the following places:

Legs shoulder width apart, down to the right, down to the left, down to the middle. Then right leg kicks and left leg kicks. Next we'll get the right quad by grabbing your right foot with your left hand and bringing it toward your butt, and switch. We'll get into a butterfly to stretch the groin, and finish in a push-up position, flexing the calves one at a time. It's that easy, and it takes no more than 3 minutes.

Go Somewhere Relaxing

I'm currently writing this in a notebook on a plane home from San Francisco, and it's obvious now, but it took this trip for me to think of this. If you want to wake up calm, go somewhere calm, a place with soothing sounds and picturesque views. As I listened to the waves of the Pacific Ocean early this morning, I realized how clearly I could think and how happy I was to be awake. There is no possible chance that being asleep an extra 15 minutes could ever lead to the sort of joy or satisfaction you get from being content in a beautiful place.

Sadly, we obviously don't all have the luxury of being near the water or the mountains. So get creative, go out and explore, find a beautiful view, a stream, a gorgeous monument. Immerse yourself in whatever it is that you can marvel at. This world is filled with intricacies that go far beyond our comprehension, so go out and appreciate them. And if you don't like going outside or if it's a day in which you can't, find an awe-inspiring video on TV, or listen to a soft sound. Whenever my friends and I didn't want to watch anything in particular, but still wanted to have something on, we watched this incredibly stunning visual documentary called *Samsara* on Netflix. If you don't feel like watching

TV, your phone is filled with apps of sounds or "white noise" that you can use to ease your mind.

Becoming curious about the world around you and having a constant itch to learn and discover are two of the most desirable characteristics imaginable. It takes courage to get outside your comfort zone and explore subjects in which you know nothing about; but the rewards are so much greater than the risks. Worst-case scenario is you tried to do something different and didn't enjoy it. Big deal, it will only be another story to tell later on. Approach things with an open mind, ask questions, but don't stress too much about the answers. The process of learning is more important than the end result.

Get yourself in a relaxed state so you're not over anxious, overwhelmed or rushed going into the day. Take it easy and settle down. You got this. But also remember, it's only step #1.

I love the 3am version of people.
Vulnerable. Honest. Real.
Anonymous drunk person

O - OPENNESS

This is going to be the longest chapter because I truly believe it is the most important. There are 2 primary components to the openness piece of your morning routine. The first is about opening up to other people, and the second is about opening up to yourself. I love routine, but I hate monotony—and this is why there are different options for each component of your 5-step process.

One of the most worthwhile traits we can portray in life is vulnerability. **Being vulnerable, asking for help, acknowledging weakness, should *never* be misconstrued as something to hide or as a sign of defeat. We must go about life asking questions, becoming curious, incessantly searching to learn and discover as much as we possibly can.**

Active Listening

I had just spent a few hours in Evanston, Illinois on my feet, talking to hundreds of people, and I had a daunting 45-minute Uber ride home because I was not in the mood to talk to one more person. I got in the car and immediately apologized that I was exhausted, and needed to close my eyes. I could tell the driver was a talker, but he reluctantly agreed and put on the radio. His music choice was intriguing, but not totally surprising for a man his age, and with his long hair. It was a combination of popular rock songs and a few I had never heard before. I had to inquire. Turns out, my driver was once a Chicago music legend, Ronnie Rice. He did the vocals, keyboard, and guitar for the band New Colony Six, which had 10 top 100 songs between 1966 and 1971.

I love music, but I am not that knowledgeable about it. I must have asked Ronnie over 100 questions that ride, and was not afraid to admit my lack of expertise, and discover from him so much about the rock and roll scene in Chicago in the early 70's (which is not something I've longed to know about, but rather was just a cool topic of conversation). Ronnie worked closely with the guys from Survivor ("Eye of the Tiger") and told me rock 'n' roll stories that you'd never believe. He's now in his 60's and still performing live events, and I never would have known any of that had I not been curious, been vulnerable, and asked about his extraordinary life.

This goes back to the theory of learning from others what you don't know, admitting that somebody is more knowledgeable than you in a particular area of life, and making it your mission to find out what that area is. Ask as many appropriate questions about it as you can to gain a sliver of their wisdom. It's a win-win: you come out with new tidbits of information, and they are able to feel pride in the knowledge they shared. We can acquire this knowledge every morning by reaching out to people who we believe can make a significant impact on our lives.

You're only going to Get COMFY with this if you start practicing. Talk to everybody. Ask the cashier at the grocery store how her day is going. Ask the restaurant worker what else she likes to do. Ask your coworkers how their weekends were or if they have any upcoming plans for the next. Get used to speaking with everyone, but more importantly, get used to really listening and responding to the answers.

Listening is such an overlooked skill, but to me, it is the most important trait we can display. President Bill Clinton is said to make you feel like *you* are the only person in the world when you speak to him. And that is when you talk to Bill Clinton, who is actually one of the most important people in the world! My friends' dad, Rob, has a story in which he bumped into Bill Clinton in a bagel store, and Bill asked him about Northwestern because he was wearing a Northwestern hat. The President was so knowledgeable about Northwestern, from the campus to the basketball team, and Rob said they chatted for 15 minutes, mainly with President Clinton just asking questions and being fascinated by what Rob had to say. It even got to the point in which Rob had to politely remove himself from the conversation, because he was running late for a meeting!

Bill Clinton intently listens to what you have to say, and thinks about how relatable he can be to you. Political beliefs aside, this is a type of person you want to be around. This is how you should aim to make people feel when you converse with them. Listening is such a gift that if used well, immediately makes you desirable to others and yourself.

Overcoming Fear and Doubt

I had a professor, Dr. Nicholas Pearce, who perfectly encouraged this vulnerability and audacity to reach out to people you never would expect to answer. In our capstone assignment, we were urged to reach out to a business executive in any industry and inquire about how their informal and formal networks influenced their business decisions.

I reached out to and successfully spoke with a CEO of one of the largest restaurant groups in Chicago and across the country. I was able to get in touch because of a mutual friend, and because of my relationship with this friend, he was not reluctant to put me in touch with a person of this magnitude. Every relationship matters, and people will only be willing to go to bat for you if they believe that you will provide a positive representation of them.

This conversation changed my life, by the way. As somebody who absolutely loves food and restaurants, I thought this would be an enjoyable discussion during which we'd touch on the topics in my paper, we'd talk food, and I'd probably end up with my stomach growling. That is essentially how the interview was going, until he turned the tables and started to focus on me. What my program was like, what they're teaching, what I wanted to do, why I wanted to do it, etc. It was fascinating to see that people are genuinely interested in you as well.

Get COMFY revealing information about yourself. He finished the conversation by offering advice to me, "You can watch all the golf videos in the world and go to the range as much as you possibly can; but it is not until you get out on the course that you are truly going to get better. The same goes for the restaurant industry." This was a pivotal moment that gave me the confidence I needed to enter the restaurant industry as my first job out of school. I cannot express enough how important and meaningful these conversations can and will be if you Get COMFY having them.

This is the email I sent so you can get a feel as to how you should structure them:

Dear _____,

_____ so generously connected me to you, expressing that you would be the perfect person to speak with regarding leadership, management, and the restaurant industry. I am a classmate and close friend of _____ from Northwestern and now at Kellogg, and I am passionate about the *restaurant industry and one day hopefully owning my own restaurant.*

I have an assignment that encourages me to reach out to executives and acquire a feel for how they have developed and utilize both their formal and informal networks to benefit themselves and their organizations.

I understand that you are an incredibly busy person, but I was wondering if we could meet sometime within the month of August, whenever is most convenient for you, to have this discussion.

I am extremely excited to learn about your career, and I look forward to hearing from you soon!

Thank You,
Jordan Gross

This is a template that you can use to reach out to somebody you want to speak with in your extended network. It is not a spray and pray method in which you copy and paste the same email and just change the names and the industries. These are person-alized, well-crafted messages that convince the other person that you are worth their time. I will break it down by paragraph:

1. **Know your audience** – The most important by far. In this paragraph, you are giving the receiver a reason as to why they should even read your email. Thus, it is best to open by first stating the name of the person that has created this mutual connection. If you do not have a mutual connection with somebody you would like to contact, find an article, an interview, or a quote that they have said, and start with that, to make them know you are genuinely interested in them and have put time and thought into how and why you are reaching out.

   Use characteristics about them that you would want to touch on during your conversation. Here, I use leadership, management, and the restaurant industry, all traits to which this person can relate. It gives them a sense of why you are reaching out and offers praise as well.

   Lastly, introduce yourself. It doesn't need to be anything lengthy. You're not trying to boast about your accolades, but rather give a brief background, a description of what exactly you want to talk about, how you received their information, and what your goal of the conversation would be. These emails should all be extremely personal, and you should not copy & paste from one email to another. Know exactly who it is you are talking to, and develop a message that most resonates with them.

2. **Be genuine** – This is the more specific reasoning for why you are reaching out, if you have one. Working on an assignment or something for school is a great way to connect with these people, as they are curious as to what is going on in universities today. Their talent comes from these universities, and they want to know what is being taught and how they can help. Trust me, you'd be surprised how many people sincerely enjoy giving advice to others. If you don't have a specific assignment like I did here, say you are working on something on your own, a project, a report, it doesn't have to be anything too specific, as long as you are respectful and not deceitful.

3. **Acknowledge their time!** – This is most likely a person with a tremendous amount on their plate, and it is admirable if they give 15-20 minutes of their day to speak

with you. Also, be on their schedule. I use the phrase, "whenever is most convenient for you" because that is honestly the truth. If a person of this stature is finding time to speak with me, I am going to make it my obligation to clear out my schedule for whenever works best for that person, not for whenever works best for me. Another way to go about this is to include a window of times that you are available so the other person can choose a slot in there, or recommend a different time. This also minimizes back and forth email exchanges.

4. **Be excited!** – Do not be afraid to show that you are eager to hear back from this person. You know they are a big deal, and so do they. Do not try to seem cool or nonchalant. Throw in a couple exclamation points, and express your enthusiasm and energy because this is what people want to see, and this is with whom people want to chat. They don't want to have the same mundane conversations that they have every day, so be refreshing, assert your curiosity, and most importantly, *prepare, prepare, prepare* for that interview once they respond!

Something I struggle with is the fear of being annoying, the anxiety that coincides with reaching out to somebody and feeling like I am pestering them. Getting COMFY has guided me and assisted me so much with overcoming this deterrent to my personal growth journey.

The way in which I previously viewed reaching out to somebody was this: I would put myself in their shoes too much and then get inside my own head about what they would think or say upon reading (and hopefully) responding to my message. "This kid is using me." "Why should I waste my time talking to him?" "Well, what do I get out of this, he's just a young kid, so probably nothing, so I won't talk to him." This is where being willing to provide value at any cost comes into the equation. Yes, I am in my early twenties with little work experience, and not nearly as much knowledge as the person I am trying to speak to. But, I am always willing to help in whatever way possible and express this to everybody with whom I speak. People love helping and feeling like people need their help. People enjoy talking about themselves when asked, so turn conversations onto them, ask questions, engage, and reap the benefits of meaningful dialogue.

Have a desire to constantly add value to everyone you encounter. Keep track of whom you speak with and one or two things about them, and update how you have improved that person's life. If you have not, keep them in mind for opportunities to help them, like they helped you, in the future. You create this entire "Life Network" but it should be more than a network. It is really a list of all your friends, the people who have influenced you, and hopefully who you have influenced as well.

Becoming Memorable

Another outstanding person to look to for this is Tim Ferriss. If you have not read *The Four-Hour Work Week* I would recommend you get your hands on it as soon as you can (but finish this first!). In it, Tim explains how he had students at Princeton reach out to top-level executives and celebrities. Tim's creative approach is fantastic, and it empowered me to not be afraid to email twice or three times, and to use various means to contact people through blogs, social media, email, phone, or in person!

One area of mine that I am working on moving forward is the quality and creativity of these conversations that I have. I am a very active listener, which I highly recommend when speaking with anyone—I truly try to absorb the answers somebody is giving and then build on the conversation based on what they are saying, rather than have a set script of questions that leads to a conversation with no flow or no personal insight. Then you can relate to what they are saying by mentioning something about you that is similar, and the conversation becomes more natural.

What I mean by creativity is not asking the same mundane questions that this person hears and responds to all the time such as, "What are your biggest strengths?" "What advice do you have for someone my age?" These are great questions and you will get valuable responses, but I would rather be unique, have a little more fun, and really make the other person think about their answers. This is a technique I also picked up from Tim Ferriss's podcast, and this is asking ordinary questions in extraordinary ways. Allow me to provide you with 10 examples of fun ways to rephrase boring questions, and still get meaningful responses that will drive conversations:

Intended meaning (Boring)	**Question (Fun!)**
1. What are your three biggest strengths?	1. What three characteristics would a commercial about you highlight?
2. What principles guide your life?	2. What would be written inside your ideal fortune cookie?
3. What are you most proud of?	3. What would your significant other say is your biggest accomplishment?
4. Who are your biggest inspirations?	4. Who are you having over for a dinner party, what are you making, and why?
5. Tell me about a weakness of yours.	5. What would you not reveal about yourself in a job interview?
6. What are your passions?	6. If you had one extra day to do anything, what would you do?
7. What do you like to read?	7. What books do you give as gifts?
8. How did you get started in your area of expertise?	8. What newspaper headline best explains the beginning of your career?
9. How have you learned from your mistakes?	
10. What advice do you have for me?	

| | 9. If you feel comfortable, can you tell me about one of the worst days of your life and how did you bounce back? |
| | 10. What do you incessantly tell your children? |

Using these types of questions is going to require courage and Getting COMFY outside your comfort zone. A strong way to begin asking questions in this way is by stating to the person that you like to think outside the box, and you enjoy being unique and having fun in the way you ask questions and converse. In my experience, it can get a bit awkward. People are taken aback, and they may initially think it is or you are strange for asking that. But when they hang up, they will remember you, you will stand out, and that should be one of your intentions for this conversation—not to simply chat, but rather to begin an ongoing dialogue. That dialogue is more likely to continue if you did something that caught their attention.

These questions may also lead to silence from the other side because they actually have to think, rather than feed you the same answer they give everybody else. This is good! Silence is good; embrace it, and Get COMFY with silence! A helpful technique to begin embracing silence is to simply state, "Feel free to take a minute to think about this one, I don't intend for it to be easy" or "Take the time you need for this question". Feel out the conversation and adapt to the personality of the other person. The more playful and creative they seem, the easier it will be to ask these questions. Those who seem more stern and by the book may make asking these questions more challenging, but it will also be more beneficial by allowing you to step outside your comfort zone.

What is the main benefit of asking these questions in this way? It is not to have a more effective conversation, because you're hoping that the answers are going to be similar to what they would be if you asked the question directly. The meaning behind these questions is that it will be more fun for you, and more fun for them, because there is thought and creativity involved. It will also provide something unique about you that hopefully the other person will remember in the thousands of conversations they have of this nature. Escape the banality of these conversations and make them your own.

Openness Advantages

The benefits of simply having a conversation, or expressing yourself to somebody else are unmatched. If you are a person that is struggling with internal issues, whether they be fear, sadness, anxiety, love, stress, do not keep them pent up! They will consume you, and your mind and body cannot handle that. You must share these thoughts and feelings with others. People will be receptive; you will not be ill-received. And if you ever are, then that is not a person you want in your life. Allow yourself to be helped. Stubbornness is not attractive!

It's a common theme among members of my family that we are very difficult patients. Whenever ill or injured, we do not like to even admit it, and we certainly do not like to be pitied or helped. It stems from resilience and our determination to overcome any roadblock, but we must understand that we do not need to overcome on our own. People are willing to help at your weak moments not to make you feel defeated, but rather to bring you back quicker to the optimal person they know you can be.

When I get hurt, my immediate reaction is always, "No, no I'm fine, I'll be okay, I don't need a doctor or anything." And then I'll go home with an ankle the size of an eggplant, my parents will scold me for trying to be a tough guy, and the delay in going to a specialist will probably set me back longer than if I had gone to somebody right away. I'm trying to show how strong and resilient I am, but in actuality it is just foolish. The first reaction to people coming to your side should be, "You know what, yes. I thought I'd be okay, but to be safe, can you take a look and see if I need a doctor?" Stubbornness is not attractive! **Be able to receive help just as easily and as well as you can provide it.**

Open up to others and they will be your best means of overcoming your internal qualms. Do not look to drugs, or alcohol, or social media, because these are addictions that are short-term solutions to long-term problems. Conversations will be ongoing, and somebody will constantly be there for you as a way to speak candidly and offer the advice and confidence you need to push forward. Get COMFY having and also receiving these conversations.

Openness Best Practices

Another unconventional practice that I truly believe works best is to **NOT** take notes during conversations. It is so important to actively listen to the other side, and note taking disassociates you from the other person. Not taking notes enhances your focus and puts you in the moment, a trick so important, especially in Getting COMFY, that forces you to be in sync with whatever you are talking about with the other person. There is more flow, you get to ask more questions, learn more, and your hand never has to cramp up from writing or typing too much.

Then, and this is the kicker, I take 15-30 minutes **AFTER** the call, meeting, coffee chat is over in order to synthesize everything that I have learned. It is more effective to take the time afterward to reflect on stories and lessons I have been told, rather than to juggle 10 things at once during the call. It also helps zero in on key takeaways because you are going to write down and remember best the bits that struck you the most. If you absolutely must take notes, jot down a few things that you cannot forget. Do not try to write every single word, for your priority is to interpret and think, not copy and transcribe.

Then, want to know a great activity to do for openness the next day? Send that person another email! Thank them so much for the valuable insights they provided for your life, express gratitude for the time they took out of their hectic day, and be creative! Relate something you've found online to the conversation you had. Send an article, a video, a talk, a photo, or an idea that refers to the conversation you had the day prior. Below is an example of a note I sent to somebody in the food industry:

Hey _____,

Great talking to you this morning. I hope you had a successful day at your restaurant opening. I'm definitely going to have to try it when I'm back in New York.

I wanted to share this article _____, which provides some cool insights on one of the potential directions/disruptions/opportunities for the industry. Also, I wrote a blog post about my experience at _____ —give it a read if you'd like. I'm attaching the doc, and here is a link to the entire blog: www.feastmode1.wordpress.com

Thanks again, all the best, and I hope to meet you in person sometime soon!

Jordan

This note affirms that I took time to actively reflect on what we talked about. I made mention to what he told me he was doing that day, I sent him something relevant to both of us, and I provided him with something that related to him and his work that I thought he would find interesting. I closed by conveying that I would like to continue the conversation and speak more in the future, and sending an article allows the discussion to move forward, because then you provide something new to comment on. It is such a simple activity to find 2 minutes to thank somebody for anything that they did. On the flip side, not thanking someone can have severe repercussions and could potentially ruin your reputation or relationship with whomever you forgot or disregarded to thank.

Valuing and Maintaining Relationships

Relationships are some of the most important things we have in life. You cannot have a fulfilling day without human interaction and connecting with another individual. Sometimes however, we lose touch due to extenuating circumstances, and we miss out on relationships that could have been mutually beneficial. Because of this, I like to use openness as a time to rekindle and foster relationships with people whom I have not touched base with in a while.

Common to the theme of this entire book, this is a simple process that does not seem like it will do anything for your mentality. But it does. Put yourself in the other person's shoes: Receiving a call, text, email, Facebook message, letter from a person that you miss is a great feeling. It lets them know you are thinking about them, are curious as to what they are up to, and it makes them appreciate your relationship.

It's unfortunately so easy to lose a friend because of a lack of communication that separates you throughout the years. It is even easier to keep a friend by saying "Hi, just checking in" every couple of months. Be courageous, be the one who puts forward the effort to maintain all of your meaningful relationships. Do right by others without ever having the expectation of receiving something in return.

The final suggestion related to opening up to other people is sending gratitude emails. Expressing gratitude is monumental in establishing self-confidence and getting comfortable in your own skin. You are acknowledging that you are a product of the people around you, and you are thanking them for having an impact in your life. It's also another factor of your life that you control, and leads to a positive outlook and feeling that you will carry for the rest of the day. Below is an email that I sent to a college professor of mine a year after I FAILED her class.

Hi Sara,

I don't know if you remember me, but I was in your Gender Economics class Fall 2015. I actually failed your class, which was the first time that has happened to me in my life.

I just want to thank you for that experience. Since that class, I have focused on perspective and overcoming adversity, and have even shared my own story of failing to help others who think getting a bad grade is the end of the world. I have achieved so much since then and have really turned what seemed like a destructive experience, into one that has only benefitted me.

I wrote about learning from failure in my essay which got me into my current Kellogg program, I talked about it in the interview that landed me my dream job, and I have shared it with friends who need a pick me up story during tough times.

So thank you again. We are all going to face extreme obstacles in our lives, and it is how we react to them and persevere through them, which determines the people we ultimately become.

All the best,
Jordan

Her Response:

Jordan,

That's quite a story of achievement. I'm very happy to hear that you have come a long way and that you turned that one failure into a story of success. It makes me very happy to know that you are trying to help others and to spread a more positive message about learning from our mistakes.

Wishing you all the best moving forward,
Sara

What that email did for me was awesome. It gave me the opportunity to prove to somebody my accomplishments, circle back on a relationship, and make somebody else happy! She must have been thrilled to receive this email (which I sent at 7:27am!) and start her day knowing that somebody was grateful for her and the influence she had on their life. If you don't want to do this for you, then do it for them! People love being appreciated. Even if they are not Getting COMFY in the morning (which they should) provide somebody else the opportunity to start their day on a positive note by making them know the positive impact they have had on your life. If you think this is strange to send to a friend, family member, friend of a friend, coach, then start by saying, "Hey, I'm trying this new thing where I reach out to unbelievable people in my life. It really helps me start my day on the right foot!" or you can say, "Don't be alarmed, I'm doing great, but I just wanted to send you this note to get both of us to have an awesome day." It will feel awkward, but it will be beneficial for the both of you in the short and long run.

Failure. It is the most feared word in the human language. In business, in school, in relationships, in life. Why? I'm not really sure, so I want to urge you to embrace failure, overcome adversity, don't be afraid to feel embarrassed, feel beaten, lose, take a risk, get shut down.

Let's do even more than not let the fear of striking out keep us from playing the game. Striking out is the largest mistake you can make as a batter. It is the large failures we are afraid of that keep us from pursuing our dreams. But it is the small mistakes, the risks we are ambivalent about but don't end up pursuing, the pop flies, the groundouts, which keep us from playing the game to our full potential. The most important lessons in life are learned at some of our lowest moments. Like I mentioned in my email, we are all going to face extreme obstacles in our lives, and it is how we react to them and persevere through them, which determines the people we ultimately become.

Techniques for Self-Openness

Being open with yourself is equally as important as opening up to other people. It is another means of expression, because writing things down and getting them out in the open is much more beneficial than having them circulate your thoughts. There are a couple of techniques available to be open and honest with yourself, and reveal what exactly is going on inside your head.

Journal

Everybody fears journaling. There is a stigma associated with keeping a "diary" these days, but it can be one of the most effective tools for self-reflection and peace of mind. Do not write on your phone, computer, tablet, or anything electronic. Put thoughts on paper and feel the sensation of what it is like to write. As a front and center representation of a millennial myself—I am constantly on my phone, emailing, writing in my notes—I am working to alleviate this technological expression with real writing, and it feels great. Put away your phone for 15 minutes when you wake up, get an alarm clock instead of using your phone so you are not tempted to check it, and write in a journal rather than on your laptop. Disconnecting from the electronic world, even if it is only just for the beginning of your day will minimize the overwhelming access to information we are plagued by in this era. You know what, it's time for another challenge . . .

"Can't" Find My iPhone Challenge

Not only is it important to relinquish the desire to use our phones as soon as we wake up, but also it is a productive exercise to practice throughout the day. Use this challenge to practice patience, interpersonal skills, communication, and creativity. Also, gain a sense of appreciation for how easy some things are today as opposed to before we had these magical rectangles in our pockets.

On occasion, I can be an idiot. On occasion, I am attached to my phone. On occasion, I have a very weak bladder. On occasion, I am so attached to my phone and am such an idiot that when my weak bladder strikes, I look at my phone as I go to the bathroom. On one particular occasion after a few drinks, I dropped my phone in the toilet while I was going to the bathroom and obviously broke it.

As mentioned, I am attached to my phone. But, that is more due to convenience rather than actual obsession. Because of this, I was almost relieved when my phone broke. No texts, no emails, no Snapchats, no stalking Facebook or Instagram, just a genuine and conscious engagement in whatever situation I was in. The next day, I had to find my way to the AT&T store and meet my parents to get a new phone. I ended up talking with and paying a friend to get me a cab (there is still some importance in carrying around cash). I arrived at the store early and had no idea when my parents were going to arrive. I chatted with the AT&T people for a few minutes, and realized my parents were running late. Ironically, I had to run to the bathroom again, so I asked the people at the front of the store to tell my parents, and I described them both, that their son was in the bathroom, and I'd meet them at the front of the store. It felt weird having to explain what my parents looked like to a stranger, without being able to show her a picture, and not being able to communicate with my parents on my own. But it was also kind of fun and allowed me to start thinking about how many seemingly straight-forward everyday tasks are facilitated by the use of technology.

Thus, this challenge was born.

1. Lose your phone

2. Just kidding, but pretend as if your phone were lost for a few hours, or if you're daring an entire day

3. Create a list of tasks you must complete *It is best to do this on a weekend so work or school obligations are not compromised

4. Tasks can and should include, meet a friend for lunch, find the post office, find the bank and deposit money, describe your friend to a stranger and have them help you find him or her, borrow somebody's phone, get across the city, the list is endless but make sure they are things that would be otherwise senseless if you had technology at your disposal

5. Count how many tasks you were able to complete

6. Do it again the next week and beat your score!

K.I.S.S. – Keep It Simple Stupid. My soccer coach growing up used to say this all the time about how we should play the game, and this is the message I am perpetually trying to relay about your morning routine and your life. The challenge above is basic, but it is essential. It is essential in practicing patience, building communicative skills, solving problems creatively, and most importantly, perspective building—not only learning, but also truly feeling what it is like to live like many others do, and realizing how easy life can be for us at times, and being grateful for that.

Gratefulness is a prime place to begin when thinking about what you should put in your morning journal. Just like we may some days be sending our gratefulness emails, build up to that by writing a few things that you are grateful for each morning.

Thanksgiving is the best holiday of the year, and we go around the table and say what we are thankful for (my grandma still thinks that I'm the most creative kid in the world for bringing this tradition to the table when I was like 5) because it allows everybody to not only open up their bellies, but also their minds and share what kind of day, month, year it has been. Do this in the morning with yourself. Express how excited you are to do something, or how proud you are of another person or yourself. These are positive messages that allow you to live in the moment and show yourself that you are in control of the feelings that you have. You cannot control situations, but you can always control your response to them.

Another activity to open up your mind and release your inhibitions is to write down your fears. Maybe slightly unconventional because we want to focus on the positives in our lives, but being honest with ourselves about everything in our lives is paramount to not only a positive, productive, stress-free mindset, but also mental health in general. One of the primary reasons people suffer from anxiety or depression is because of secrets they have bottled up inside of them. It is one thing to not feel totally comfortable sharing them with somebody else immediately (although this is the goal), but at least sharing them with yourself by writing them down in a safe place is the first step to becoming comfortable with all of your emotions, fears, anxieties, self-doubts, and insecurities.

Write a letter to yourself. It does not have to be long, but think about some of the things that are holding you back in life. Take time to write out how these seemingly detrimental activities can actually be viewed as positives for either your past or future, and how and why you should be grateful for this opportunity as compared to somebody else. I want you to do this because our mindset is about perception and context. We can turn any negative into a positive if we think about our lives relative to the billions of other scenarios we could be in.

"Jane is miserable at her job because she is not doing what she enjoys"—this is a classic complaint for anybody in the working world. Merely given that sentence, I can already see a few different ways to recreate that scenario and turn it into something positive.

1. Jane has a job

2. Jane is at least doing something

3. Jane has discovered something that she does not enjoy, which can only help her find what she does enjoy next

We need to start believing all experiences are learning experiences, even the negative ones. Restructuring your thought process to reflect positivity is critical to coping with experiences that are not up to the standards we desire. Surround yourself with perspective creating events. Watch a documentary about underprivileged youth, go out and feed the homeless, visit an impoverished area. The epitome of diverse experience and a diverse life is escaping the bubble you believe is your normal reality, and immersing yourself in the lives and cultures of those that are far different from you. Once you see and even better experience how other people, maybe less, maybe even more fortunate than you live, it will become much easier to smile about whatever situation you find yourself, and realize that true comfort lies within your ability to reinvent the way you look at seemingly negative experiences.

My Openness Story

It is now my turn to round out this section by opening up to all of you. If you know me well this may come as a surprise, maybe not. This is probably the first time I have shared this with anyone, so I hope I am able to fully articulate exactly how I feel.

The Dix Hills Thunder was and is the best, most fun, most meaningful team or collaboration that I have ever been a part of. Not only was this my soccer team from age 5 to 15, but also this was my life, my dreams, my purpose, for all of these years. Soccer didn't work out for me unfortunately, but that's a different story. I can talk about every player to ever come across this team and their families for hours in the highest regard, but I'll get to the main purpose.

We were one of the best teams in the entire country—4 time State champions, 2 time Regional champions, National Bronze Medalists. Needless to say, we didn't lose very often. But every time we did, I immediately found myself hiding my emotions, *trying to conceal them inside of me, really only for my parents to ever deal with, and I rarely even opened up to them. I was an extremely competitive person, but you'd never know that because I was afraid to reveal it. I got sad, I got angry, I cried, I hurt.*

A memory that my friends and I laugh about now is that whenever I would lose, whether it was with the Dix Hills Thunder, at basketball camp, at bowling, at mini golf, at Wii tennis even, I would always pour water over my head so that it never seemed like I was crying, or looked like I was upset. It's funny to think about—a chubby little kid with long hair, pouring water on his head when he is clearly crying. But that was my scapegoat. I would get very quiet and never speak to anyone if I was upset. I never wanted to show others my weaknesses.

I'm still working on this. I am no longer nearly as competitive outwardly, but I am still competitive with myself, constantly craving improvement in everything I do, measuring myself against past and optimal performance. It's no longer water over my head, but I now mask my attitude toward undesirable outcomes with a half smile or a quick laugh, which are illustrations of me dictating how I should react to the situation, but they are not sincere. I'm still quiet when things bug me, contemplating internally rather than facing conflict outwardly and expressing disdain, worries, or doubts. This is not healthy, and I know I have to Get COMFY in sharing my thoughts with others even if I think they show signs of weakness.

I often feel like I have to put on a façade that I am so nice, caring, passionate, happy, never in a bad mood. And don't get me wrong those things are true! But that is 99% of the time. The other 1% however, nobody gets to see. If you feel like me in any way, I get it; it's daunting to reveal sides of you that may seem out of the ordinary. But please, understand that forthright expression is one of our greatest assets. It not only allows us to be free of negative sentiments, but also allows others to understand what makes us tick, and hopefully allows them to work around those nuances moving forward. We must set aside our egos, no matter how big, and be open with others and ourselves. **Overcoming the fear of failure, the fear of mistakes, the fear of embarrassment, the fear of losing, and expressing vulnerability in a way that is justifiable are the most crucial aspects of self-expression and the primary factors in living life stress-free.**

I've always believed fitness is an entry point to help you build that happier, healthier life. When your health is strong, you're capable of taking risks. You'll feel more confident to ask for the promotion. You'll have more energy to be a better mom. You'll feel more deserving of love.
Jillian Michaels

M - MOVEMENT

As you know, I was a bit heavy growing up. When all the other 6-year olds were asking for chickie fingies and fries, I was ordering foie gras and pomme frites. But I wasn't always such a snob when it came to food, I loved it all, and in great quantities too. Every time I went to California Pizza Kitchen I would have a full order of Rigatoni Marinara, piled with cheese, an entire Hawaiian pizza, no pineapple, add extra bacon, and wrap up with a Chocolate Lava Cake. Not to mention I would also finish whatever everybody else was eating, and not leave a morsel on any plate. That *probably put me back at over 3,000 calories, and over 150 grams of fat for one meal! That's almost twice as much as I should have been eating for an entire day!*

So obviously with this ambitious appetite came some weight issues. At around 16 years old, with a decent sports career, and the maturity to start realizing that my body, my emotions, and my life could all spiral downhill if I continued these eating habits, I decided to start focusing more on exercise and my diet, and the amazing impact it has on one's entire well-being. It's safe to say that now I am as healthy as ever, I am a NASM certified personal trainer, and I have even co-created a blog called Feast Mode, that describes meals out that I have enjoyed, and matches them with formidable workouts to burn off everything I ate the day prior. Movement is so important to me and it is a part of my life everyday whether it is 5 minutes or 5 hours, and it should be for you too.

Everybody tells you all about exercising for a certain amount of time each day from a very young age because it is important for your health. Well for one, they, whoever they are, are right. But two, I wish they were a little more specific. For me it is so much more than looking good and being healthy. I look fine and am quite healthy. But what movement mainly does is enhance my mental clarity. It kick starts my thinking process in the morning, allows my brain to start functioning, my body to start moving, and my thoughts to start formulating. In light of this book encouraging you to do what is necessary to get yourself COMFY with whatever gets thrown at you in your day or in your life, this has to be the most attractive quality of moving. The more you move, the more you brain moves, and the more your brain moves, the better everything else functions in your body.

Movement Methods

I have two main practices for movement in the morning. One is going to the gym and the other is going on a walk or run. Depending on what I am looking to get out of the day and out of the morning, I choose which I want to perform, and then have a series of other activities that go along with them. In both instances however, I am in a state of euphoria. I'm focusing on myself and living in the moment, which is exactly what we are aiming to accomplish.

Running

Left, right, left right left. This is the sound of movement. The cadence Marines sing as they march about. The rhythm that gets them in the right mindset, one of camaraderie and unity, that allows them to be ready for battle. We need to establish this mindset for our own personal battles, and going on a run is a great way to do so. Going on a run can either be put in this category, or our Calm section, because it is such a meditative process. It develops a state of freedom, a state of ease, and a state of self-reflection as you move step by step in whatever direction, to whichever location you are pursuing.

Go on a run to somewhere tranquil. Allow your body and mind to wander. Listen to your steps, listen to your breath, and listen to the amazing thoughts you will be able to create in such a state of ease. When I run, I use it as a time for thought creation. Some of my best ideas (what I perceive to be my best ideas) have come to me while on a run. The idea for this book came to me while I was on a run!

And do not fear if you are unwilling to or unable to run. Walking works just as well! Often times I will be sore, so I throw in my headphones and start walking outside with absolutely no agenda, and I get the same effect as if I were jogging. Walking around aimlessly is something that may feel unnatural to you, even though it is so basic. It is a great exercise to practice to start learning how to insert yourself into foreign or seemingly uncomfortable situations.

When I run, I am attempting to generate thoughts, or even more of the goal, thoughts will generate naturally based on my observations. But a helper is listening to podcasts. As I mentioned earlier, I'm a big podcast guy. I like to listen to people speak about their lives, how they became successful, why they became successful, and what they do every day to ensure they continue that success. I develop my own ideas from these talks, and pick and choose best practices that I believe will most fit in with my life. This is exactly what I want you to do with this book! Below are a few of my favorite podcasts to get my mind moving:

1. *How I Built This* – A thought-provoking, well-crafted show that has NPR host Guy Raz sit down with the world's greatest innovators, business leaders, and all around people. Great for the entrepreneural mind, or anybody inspired by grit, perseverance, and overcoming adversity.

2. *Achieve Your Goals with Hal Elrod* – Hal Elrod, one of the primary motivations for this book, is all about positivity and optimism. He speaks with members of his Miracle Morning community and others who have overcome hardship to achieve extraordinary goals.

3. *Girlboss Radio with Sophia Amoruso* – This podcast beautifully illustrates the phrase "girl power". Sophia Amoruso, founder of Nasty Gal, interviews the world's most amazing female leaders and has wonderful conversations about how and why they do what they do.

4. *The Tony Robbins Podcast* – Tony Robbins is amazing. Truly one of my heroes with the way he is able to influence, persuade, and inspire. He interviews some of the world's greatest leaders from all different walks of life, and shows the audience what it takes to achieve tremendous feats.

5. *The Tim Ferriss Show* – I couldn't get out of here without mentioning Tim Ferriss. Tim sits with many of the most recognizable names in sports, entertainment, politics, and business, and dissects what

exactly puts them on a different playing field than the average person.

Moving in the form of running, jogging, or walking is paramount to my mental state and I truly believe that the more you start to move, the more you will start to think, and the more you start to think, the more ideas you will generate, and the more ideas you generate, the more ideas you will pursue, and the more ideas you pursue, the more chances you will have to Get COMFY!

Gymming

Alternatively, I also like to move in the form of weightlifting or going to the gym and working out. Whereas going on a run allows me to Get COMFY thinking, going to the gym is suitable for when I kind of want to think about nothing. This is all about living in the moment, not becoming overwhelmed with what may be nerve-racking for the remainder of the day. It is a time for me to get laser focused on myself, on an activity that is grueling and demanding, and prove to myself that I can accomplish seemingly impossible feats. Other tasks throughout the day should seem easy in comparison to exercises I just finished. It's something that I know is under my control. So many things in life are not under your control, but doing this is, completing a workout is, and feeling positive about it is.

When I'm in the gym, I'm in the zone, a safe place I know I can explore without being judged or having to be anybody but myself. I go there to experience nothingness. Just the feeling of doing something that gets my body going. For this reason, I don't usually listen to podcasts when I'm lifting at the gym, but rather, it will be the one time I listen to music on my headphones. I don't have to focus on any lessons to be learned or stories to be told, but can melt into the songs and stay zeroed in on my workout. I'm not a knowledgeable music guy like I said, so I won't give you recommendations as to what I listen to, but I will say to put something on shuffle, so you don't have to toggle with the music throughout and can just let the music and the workouts flow.

For Better or Worse

I woke up one morning and foolishly checked my email first thing. I had recently had a final round interview at Google, a dream job of mine, and was way too anxiously waiting to hear a response. Well, I did on that morning, and it wasn't the response I was looking for. Instead of complaining, getting angry, getting frustrated, I decided to Get COMFY. I ferociously ran to the gym and started a heavy lift, exploding through different workouts, hitting and kicking the bag, releasing all that pent-up disdain I had for what had just occurred. It was one of the best workouts I had ever had.

Fast-forward a year and I had received a job offer to Hillstone Restaurant Group, a new dream position of mine. I decided to Get COMFY again. I trotted to the gym and used the workout to celebrate my emotions, to embrace my accomplishment. I was moving a mile a minute, going through each machine without a care in the world.

I juxtapose these stories to reveal that going to the gym is advantageous for a variety of situations. The gym is my escape from disappointment, my palace for triumph. When you use the gym to Get COMFY in the morning, it will allow you to feel exactly how you want to feel. It is solely you, the weights, and the workout, and you are in total control.

Don't think you have to go to the gym, or even get out of your house to get moving! If the weather is crappy, or if you don't belong to a gym, then enjoy a workout from the comfort of your own home! There are dozens and dozens online, but below is one that I use often.

1. 25 sit-ups

2. Jump to your feet

3. 25 jumping jacks

4. 25 high knees

5. 25 push-ups

It's much more about getting your blood and brain going, than it is the severity of the workout. At the same time, feel free to make it your exercise for the day and do a full session.

Athlete Testimonials

But don't only listen to me when it comes to the importance of movement.

Movement and exercise have been the building blocks and foundation of not just my fitness but my entire athletic career as well. Many people don't see the amount of exercise and training put in by athletes as it is, but the extra work a select few do is hard to notice. I would argue that the extra, "off-time" training that few athletes do is the difference between being good and great in one's respective field or sport. For instance, on the football team at Northwestern, I noticed one of our best defensive linemen always staying late after organized workouts to get a little extra work. It might be grip work one day and core strength another. But after four years of this, he would be drafted and earn his way onto the 53-man roster of the Green Bay Packers.

While not everyone might have making the NFL as a goal to strive for when they workout, I think it's important to set goals regardless. Going into the gym without goals is like driving to your in-laws from out of state without a GPS. You need a tangible plan to set yourself up for success. I've experienced goal-oriented success personally and would encourage anyone who has lifted a weight, run a sprint or sipped a healthy Jamba Juice smoothie to seek the same.

This was written by Austin Carr, a Northwestern football legend, who currently plays with the New Orleans Saints. Austin was the Big Ten Receiver of the Year in 2016. He led the conference in receiving yards, touchdowns, and receptions, received All-American honors, and set Northwestern all-time records in both receiving yards and touchdowns. It was an absolute honor getting to know Austin in our year together at Kellogg, as he was not only one of the best football players I have ever gotten to know, but he also was one of the best people I have ever met. Some of the things you can hear people saying about him are, "This kid could do anything he wants in life." "He could be the president one day!" "How is he so amazing at football, singing, acting, and anything else he tries?!" "He is such a perfect human being." Austin certainly embodies these characteristics.

Austin mentions a goal-oriented process when it comes to his fitness regimen. This is exactly what you should be doing, and I want to add to it. Attainable goals are such a cliché term, but these are the goals you should be setting. Things that you know are difficult, but can be accomplished. The word goal can be so daunting. Combat this by calling them milestones, or visions, that you are striving to reach.

He also mentions this "off-time" training that separates the good from great athletes. This is the ticket. Being the first person to practice, being the last one to leave. In Getting COMFY, we have the same mindset. The great people are going to be those that take the extra time to focus on themselves and Get COMFY. These are the ones that know it is important, like athletes, to put in the added effort, passion, and determination that the majority does not have. Those who Get COMFY are the ones who can be like Austin in all different facets of their lives. These are the super humans, the select few who use this unrelenting mindset to achieve inexplicable feats.

But hey, maybe you're not an American Football fan, and you have a bit more of a global perspective. You love futból (soccer), the world's best sport (sorry Austin) and the world's most beautiful game. Jake Freeman and I have been playing soccer together since age 5. Rivals to begin, we called each other "butthead" or "poopface" as we tried to lead our teams to peewee victory. But rivals soon turned to teammates, teammates turned to friends, and 17 years later, Jake and I could not be closer.

Jake is the best soccer player I have ever played with. In high school he led the nation in scoring and earned both All-Region and All-State honors. In college as a freshman, he was impressive enough to earn All-League honorable mention, and by his senior year he was a unanimous First Team All-League selection, leading his team in scoring. Oh, and did I mention this league was the Ivy League?

And this team was Harvard University? Yea, Jake is a pretty smart guy as well, graduating Harvard with a degree in Sociology. Let's hear from another star athlete about what movement has done for his life.

It's no secret that moving our bodies is important for our overall health. We read all the time, about the "irrelevant" and "exaggerated" facts that say "studies show people that sit X amount of hours during the day are Y percent more likely to suffer from this, this and this." And although these facts can be frustrating to hear, especially if you work long hours sitting at a desk, that does not mean they can be ignored.

While it wouldn't be realistic or healthy to track the hours we spend sitting, standing, walking, moving, etc. . . . The truth is that we, as human beings, need to be up and about, moving around, as much as we possibly can.

But, before we get into the "why" of just how important activity and exercise are, let me start you off with a simple tip to begin your morning routine that will shockingly change your day-to-day life (as it has changed mine). You'll do this before you even start to Get COMFY. You'll do this before you get into any calming practices or begin opening up for the day. And what's great about this is that it's extremely straightforward.

Whatever time you set your morning alarm for, as soon as it goes off and your eyes open, the first thing you do is put your two feet on the ground

That means before you look at your phone, before you even turn off the alarm, you already have your two feet on the ground and are then standing up. This is our first "movement" of the day and, oh boy, it is a crucial one.

It doesn't seem like that big of a deal. Maybe you're thinking, "Ok this sounds good in theory but it really doesn't change anything or help make my day better." It may sound that way. I won't deny that. I felt the same about it. But after trying it once and then getting into a rhythm of doing it day in and day out, I promise that you will never hit the snooze button again and you will feel more awake each and every morning from this one change.

As an athlete waking up for morning practices, I felt a significant difference in my energy level for training before and after I decided to integrate this first step into my morning routine. There was no more irritation of waking up at 6am, no more sluggishly crawling out of bed after trying to get an extra ten minutes of sleep, and no more poor starts to my day. I was right up onto my two feet, feeling good and ready to get to the next part of my routine.

So if you're someone who isn't a morning person, do me a favor and give it a try. You'll be surprised just how big of an impact such a small change can make.

***

Why do we exercise? Why is it important for us to be active? If I'm not training to compete in the New York City Marathon, why should I feel the need to go out and do a cardio workout every day?

This isn't about what we need to do. This is about us taking the 24 hours we're privileged to have each day and setting ourselves up to feel our absolute best, so we can be successful in every daily task that may come our way. I'm not here telling you to cut down on the hours you work or to push you to think about becoming the next American Ninja Warrior. All I want is for you to think about your body and understand how vital movement is to us in leading our best lives and becoming the best versions of ourselves.

The benefits of being active and exercising are endless. Yes, we're all aware of that in general. But let's dive into what exactly we get out of moving our bodies.

1) Physical shape: The obvious one. No need to go on and on about it.

Whether it is the main reason or not, all of us work out to become more physically fit. Just as we strive to be the best we can in the professional working world, we also want to improve and better our bodies. Our motives may be different. For some, say parents for example, exercise could be a priority because they want to be fit to play and interact with their children. For athletes, activity and training is paramount to be able to compete at the highest level in their sports. And for others, exercise can be appearance driven with the desire to have our bodies look good. Each individual's drive will vary. But we all, for one reason or another, would like to be more physically fit or in better shape than the day before and activating our bodies gives us the best chance to do that.

2) Mentally: Likely the most important benefit of exercise leading to success in other parts of our lives.

I'm a soccer player, who has been on some of the best teams in the nation and has played at the highest level his whole life. So having been put through some incredibly difficult workouts through the years, with 20 to 25 others doing it with me, I know I'm not alone in feeling this way . . .

There is no better feeling in the entire world than taking on a workout so intense, that you had no idea you could actually do, and absolutely crushing it. That feeling after finishing, after your body has been pushed to its full limit, is a feeling that's unmatched. Long distance runners call it runners high, so we can refer to it as a workout or exercise high.

I hope most of you know what I'm talking about, some of you have experienced this feeling at one point in your life, and the rest of you, you are salivating waiting to give this a try. I highly recommend trying to challenge your body in this kind of manner. The end result might even change your outlook on exercising overall, for the better.

I'll never forget the most strenuous session of training I've ever been a part of. I was a college freshman, arriving on campus for the first time. With my first preseason soccer practice set for the next day at 6:30 am, I was full of excitement. When I arrived at the locker room that morning, I would soon learn we wouldn't be touching a ball the whole two-hour session. But then I was also told it wasn't going to be a fitness or track workout. So then what were we going to do for my first practice as a Division 1 soccer player? Our 25 players were eagerly waiting for the coaches to arrive, and in walked Sergeant Mark Tribus of the United States Marines. Mark then informed us he would be leading the team through a two-hour marines boot camp for the morning session. At that moment, you could hear the stomach drop of each and every player. Our coaches walked in and said let's get to it. When we arrived at the field, waiting for us were army tanks, camouflage weighted vests, hundred millimeter rifles, and 150-pound tires.

I won't bore you with too many details, but after that first hour of bear crawling through obstacles with weighted vests on, climbing over tanks, and doing reps and reps of every possible army workout you could think of, both my legs and arms were on fire from the pain. But the hardest part was still to come. The beginning was (somewhat) tolerable. The second half of the training was where it got real.

We walked over to the Charles River, which was going to be our racetrack. Tribus explained the details to us. "There are going to be times when a teammate of yours is tired, and you'll have to carry their weight . . . so today we are literally going to carry each others' weight." It was five of us per team, five to a stretcher. The course was set up all the way around the river, measured to be about an hour long. And our task was for four people to hold one handle of the stretcher each, and run as fast as we could while one teammate lay on top of it, racing the other groups around the river. Here, it's worth noting that simply running around the Charles River once, just by yourself, would be a good workout. Now we were expected to round the river multiple times, while carrying another individual. And as if that wasn't grueling enough, there were check points throughout the course where we would have to stop and each team member would have to do 50 push-ups and then get right back on our feet and back to running with the stretcher.

To give you a little bit of perspective of how I was feeling, at the 5-minute mark I already felt like dropping to the floor and passing out. To this day I still can't quite fathom how I got through it. But, after 60 freakin minutes, when I crossed that finish line, (after nearly puking and resisting the urge to jump in the river out of exhaustion) the most unbelievable feeling of bliss passed through me. I felt like I had conquered the world.

I had that high without a doubt. I thought my body had reached its limit too many times during that task, mission, torture, whatever you want to call it. But that sensation of accomplishment I had afterwards was something out of a movie and ended up being worth every ounce and second of pain.

Are there great, rewarding feelings that come from achieving an academic feat or task at work? Absolutely. But it doesn't quite compare to the feeling we get after achieving something we set ourselves out to do with real physical exertion of energy. That feeling is second to none.

***

3) Energy and Health:

Now, it is true that this feeling after an incredible workout is something we crave and can be a motive for us to exercise as much as possible. And sometimes, thinking about that feeling of reward might even help push us through our most tedious and exhausting workouts. But, more importantly, it is what those workouts do for us hours later that allows us to be so efficient, effective and full of energy for the rest of our day. Activating, strengthening, and then exhausting our bodies will let us excel moving forward in the coming hours. We feel fulfilled, accomplished, content with the work we have put our bodies through and goals we achieved earlier in the day.

Energy levels. Go through your normal week of exercising every, or every other day and then go the next week without hitting the gym, playing a sport, or going for a walk/run. Then look back and think about which week you felt like you had more energy throughout the day. I guarantee the first week when you kept your body active you were far more alert at work, felt way more energetic when you got home, and had a desire to cook meals, attend social gatherings, etc. Obviously we don't want to take long stretches of days without working out, but just to really gauge an understanding and see what I mean, take those 3 days and lay low and then tell me how you feel.

I try to workout, or play a sport everyday, twice a day if I can. It's become a habit. If I haven't been active in a day and got my body moving, I don't feel right. By no means am I saying you need to be the same way. I just want you to think about getting out there and exercising more days than not or as much as you possibly can. That is the step we want to take to eventually implement movement into our daily routine.

Health:

Bottom line is—staying active and exercising daily keeps the body feeling more energetic each day and throughout the grind of a full week. Not only will our bodies feel more upbeat, but our minds will also be sharper from that morning workout, later on in the day. Whether you are a student or an employee, you'll be more engaged in that school assignment or company meeting that afternoon. Activating our bodies earlier improves our creativity and enhances brain activity. The more active your body is, the more active your brain is.

But what does this mean for our overall health? We want to take care of our bodies. We want to live longer. Exercising is the first step that allows us to do both of those things. But the best part is, being active naturally causes us to want to make healthier choices for ourselves in all aspects of life, like eating cleaner. Getting COMFY and waking up early to go through a proper and efficient morning routine are crucial for your health. That structure, combined with pushing yourself through a workout and being energized during the rest of the day will have your body and mind tired by the end of it. It will allow you to get into a regimented sleeping schedule, which is so important for your recovery the next day, but also for your long-term health.

4) Outlet: A crucial part of movement. There is more to it than just the action being done.

Outlet from stresses. I'm not an extremely stressed person, but I do understand that everyone is different and stress can be a heck of a beast for people to deal with. If you fall into that category, where you feel very stressed throughout the day, then I strongly recommend making exercise your friend.

Even though I didn't feel extremely stressed on most days at school, between academics, clubs, social life, meetings with professors, etc., there was still a ton of action going on each day at Harvard. So as part of a soccer team of 30, there were going to be some guys coming into practice stressed out whether it was from an upcoming exam or maybe a completely separate personal matter. The point is, our team and coaching staff would always say, "no matter what is going on across the river (regular campus and athletics were on opposite sides of the Charles River) let's use the two hours of practice we have here today to get away from all of that, clear our minds, and make ourselves better." Practice each day, or any midweek game acted as an outlet from our stresses or, so to speak, a "break" from real life. And it works. It's the truth. As we began practice and the ball started to move, all thoughts of tests, classes and any other worries were nonexistent.

And the same can happen for you too. If you've had a tough few days at work, or maybe had an argument with your significant other or a family member, I encourage you to use exercise as your temple. Go on that early morning run. Get that big mid day lift in to forget about work for a few hours. You might say, "Well what does it really matter, I'll start thinking about all this stress right after working out." Yea, you might. But you'll also learn to love those few hours in which your mind is completely free and clear and you can focus on what your body is doing. Exercise is our outlet. Movement can be the answer to oh so many things.

Obviously, I strongly believe that exercising and moving our bodies are critical towards us living our best and happiest lives. I'm a prime example.

I am my happiest and have my most daily success when I am constantly active. If there is anything I can leave you with it's this: make it your goal to be more active than you were the day, week or month before. Let's make movement one of the most enjoyable parts of Getting COMFY so we can feel great for the rest of our day and for the rest of our lives.

I mean, wow. You can't express any better than that how important movement is for our lives. There is seriously nothing I can even add to Jake's remarks so I'll just say this. Take it from a Harvard athlete and one of Harvard's greatest soccer players, student-athletes, and people of all time, that Getting COMFY, and especially moving, is essential for all areas of life.

So you've heard from me, and you've heard from 2 sensational people about what moving does for their lives. I want to offer one more option and promote a fantastic movement that coalesces perfectly with the Getting COMFY mindset: Zumba. I heard the founders speak on you guessed it, a podcast (*How I Built This*), and I was instantly impressed and hooked by the concept and overall message it offers. Anybody can do it.

In the late 1990's and early 2000's three Alberto's created a movement. They wanted people to workout, but they also wanted people to smile and have fun while doing it. Zumba comes from the word "rumba" which means party in Colombia where the dance fitness craze originated. People come to dance for an hour and rid their minds of anything negative. They merely focus on the moves and magic of the music.

When the 2008 financial crisis hit, Zumba exploded. While so many other businesses crashed, Zumba classes were packed. People decided that in this low point in their lives, they were going to start climbing back by being happy for one hour. Every single person in the class is smiling. Just like Getting COMFY, Zumba is something that members do for themselves because they want to do it, not because they have to do it. That's all it takes to get your mindset on track.

FEJ: Freeing Electrifying Joy is the epitome of a Zumba class. 20 minutes in, the music takes over, and the person is fully liberated. This is the aim for Zumba and this is the aim for Getting COMFY. **Fully entrench yourself with thoughts and actions that are most meaningful and beneficial to you, and all the stress, trouble, and worry will disappear. And even if it is** just for a moment, and the worries come back, you are now realizing that they are possible to overcome.

From there to here and here to there,
funny things are everywhere.
Dr. Seuss

F - FUNNY

"Hi pretty lady, I'm David, what is your name?"
"What, what is he saying to me?" she yells. "I'm
excited to have you here in my home, I wonder
what I did to deserve such a treat." he replies. "I
don't want a treat David, we're about to sit down
for dinner!" "We're having dinner together?
Yippee! Lucky me!" "What are you lucky about?
Did you win the lottery or something?" "With you,
I did."

This seems like an adorable conversation between
two elderly people, and that is exactly what it was.
It's so sweet, and the man has tremendous wit and
charm that would woo any lady. This is exactly how
my grandpa spoke to my grandma. The only
problem in this scenario was that he was speaking
to the wrong grandma!

We were having holiday dinner at my grandparents' house, same as we did every year, except this time, my grandfather on my dad's side was a year into an Alzheimer's diagnosis and my grandmother on my mom's side was adjusting to her hearing loss with her new hearing aids. These conditions were devastating for our family. But, in that moment at dinner, as my brother and I watched the situation unfold, and sat their mortified as our grandpa hit on the wrong grandma, and our other grandma had no idea what was happening, we couldn't help but smile and burst out into laughter. **Finding time to laugh, or more importantly just finding time to smile in any circumstance completely adjusts your mindset, and provides a greater opportunity to better cope with any situation.**

Look for Laughs, but Smiles will Suffice

Alzheimer's is no laughing matter and neither is losing your hearing (well, I mess around with my grandma all the time about not hearing, or no longer having her teeth, but that's a different story). But, can it be? I'd argue that as long as it is not insensitive or ill hearted, comedy is one of the greatest means of escape in caring for a person with Alzheimer's, or any related illness.

I decided to dive into the "care partner" world (it is better to use this than care taker, because you are both in it together) when my grandpa was diagnosed with Dementia years ago. I volunteered at Mather Pavilion in Evanston, Illinois every Wednesday, so I could fully grasp how best to treat Grandpa David. It is remarkable the amount of patience, fluidity, creativity, compassion, and comfort one must master when with somebody with Alzheimer's. The most prominent lesson to consider is to constantly live in the moment. It is unclear what the person will remember in the next, so commit to being as present and focused as possible in the current one.

In absorbing this lesson, I made it my own goal to create as many smiles as possible in my time with each and every patient. It's like the "yes and" rule in Improv—you just go with whatever is thrown at you and allow your mind to outwardly explore your thoughts. It was almost like describing to each other our imaginations, our wildest dreams. In one conversation I was the right hand man of a world-renowned submarine captain, and in the next I was the niece (my hair was kind of long back then, don't ask and just go with it like I did) of a famous makeup artist. One woman would scream, "Oh my! It's Clark Gable! I can't believe it; I need your autograph Mr. Gable!" I didn't even know who that was, but every time I walked through the door, I was ready to give her my autograph and talk about my acting career. I'd take on whatever persona they envisioned to provide the maximal experience and number of giggles, laughs, and smiles as humanely possible. **Smile until your face starts to hurt.**

How do we tie this back to Getting COMFY? It's back to living in the present, focusing on what is right in front of you rather than the hardships, worries, or fears that are further away. I urge you to do something funny in the morning to get out of the mindset that all of life is so serious. Do not take yourself so seriously all the time, and find time to laugh at something silly and laugh at yourself. Especially in the time we live in today, the news is oversaturated with stories of tragedy. The majority of people will wake up, check the news and find stories of horror, and it's no wonder why they feel uncomfortable or pessimistic when approaching the rest of the day. Instead, wake up, and check your PNN rather than CNN.

PNN – Positive News Network

The name is corny, but it was too easy not to use, and it's all about simplicity when Getting COMFY. Creating a positive news network, mediums to make you laugh rather than cringe can fundamentally change the way you view the world and yourself. We are living in a volatile time in human history, as evidenced and reported by major news networks. The news may be overly focused on the negative because there is so much fear and terror surrounding us, but there is also plenty of good going on as well. Because of this, I created my own Positive News Network—a series of sites, videos, and stories that highlight societal advancements, heartwarming tales, and comical accounts. These are just a few of the sites I use, and I change them each day. Some days I view one, some days three. Some days I feel like I need a little more positivity in my life so I'll spend 20 minutes on my PNN, while other days I'll spend 2 minutes. Get to know yourself and your mood when you get up, and the process will become more natural.

1. **The Onion** – Satire provides the spin we are looking for to understand negative situations, but reevaluate them in a

whimsical manner. The Onion will keep you up to date on your news, but it will also make you laugh. They're quick reads, and usually the titles are funny enough to get you giggling about any worldly event.

2. **People are Awesome** – These are videos that highlight the unimaginable skills and feats humans can accomplish. From skydiving from outside of our atmosphere, to blowing bubbles with your tush, the unthinkable things people can do will get you oohing and aahing and definitely get your adrenaline going enough to put a grin on your face.

3. **Faith in Humanity** – These are not necessarily as funny as the others, but this allows you to fully engulf yourself in some of the worlds most touching moments. These are your "Soldier surprises family" or "Monkey remembers owner from 10 years ago" videos that get you to choke up in all the best ways. And the best part about these is that no matter how many times you watch them, you still get the same feeling! I just smiled and let out a weird noise thinking about the Christian the Lion video, and I know you did too!

4. **Interesting s word** – This is one of a ton of Facebook channels that, for lack of a better term, show you some really interesting shit. You'll laugh, be surprised, be inspired, and even be grossed out at times by the inventions, discoveries, and advancements people are making around the world.

I'm not saying that it's unnecessary to stay informed on current events. It is critical actually. I'm arguing that it is not a wise decision to focus on horrid stories right when you wake up, and have that taste of disgust linger for the entire day. Check the news after your day is over, discuss it over dinner, but don't allow it to consume you by reading it first thing. You know what, it's time for another challenge.

No News Challenge

I once heard somebody say that they only learned the news from other people. I am terribly sorry that I forgot whoever said this, but I am going to create a game out of your amazing words of wisdom and explanation.

1. Do not read the news at all in the morning, or throughout the day

2. Ask people about what is happening around the world in politics, sports, entertainment, business, technology, etc.

3. Write down the stories you are told

4. At the end of the day or right before bed, check the news and see how many of the top stories you became aware of, even though you did not pick up a newspaper or read a single article

You may feel uncomfortable doing this—asking somebody about the news, immediately becoming the student in a conversation. But as we learned in making ourselves vulnerable, asking people questions gives them a feeling of empowerment, and as long as we are comfortable empowering people, which we should be, we both win. We get the news, and they get the feeling like they taught somebody something.

Watch or Listen to Something Funny

This is another one of those "IDUHS" we spoke about earlier. It's almost too immature and easy to be true, but watch a short clip of something nonsensical that gets you laughing out loud. Starting to sound like a broken iPod here, but it's similar to the goal of lifting weights. We want to engage in something we do not need to think about so heavily. We want to be entirely immersed in that video, not thinking about emails or calls or meetings. It is a foolproof way to not take the day or yourself too seriously. Everybody has a different sense of humor, so please learn, discover, and share clips that make you laugh, but below are a few of my go-to sites for instant grinification.

1. **Ellen DeGeneres** — Ellen is one of the funniest people alive, and her show is so light-hearted and invites some of the most smile-worthy people on this earth to each episode. Ellen has won the Presidential Medal of Freedom for instilling not only joy in all of her viewers, but also the belief that everybody has the capability of being funny, and any situation has comedic value. A lot of her segments with children are painfully funny, and any challenge she

does with the audience has me cracking up as well.

2. **Funny Animal Videos** – I feel as if I'm a 5-year old describing this section, but any sort of video that involves a cute puppy, kitty, monkey, otter, or any other animal doing basically anything will have me laughing out loud. This is the point though—we want to get back to feeling like a kid again with thoughts that excite us and actions that provide us with the opportunity to be our honest selves.

Think about dogs for a second. They are the prime example of the realm of thought we are aiming to attain in our Getting COMFY routine. Their purpose is to make us smile, help us, and be by our sides at all times. Dogs are constantly comfortable in every situation, they do not care what anybody or "anybuddy" else thinks of them because they are content in whatever situation as long as they have a companion. Thinking about dogs and what they do for people will always bring a smile to your face.

3. **Pardon My Take presented by Barstool Sports with Big Cat, PFT,**

and Hank – I often combine M and F and listen to this hysterical podcast while I go to the gym or take a walk. I'm a big sports fan, and these guys combine sports and comedy better than anybody I have ever heard. If I don't have time for their full hour long episodes, I will watch clips on their YouTube channel or on social media of them knowingly and acceptingly acting like the greatest of imbeciles with each other and with their awesome guests.

Entertain yourself with what you know you love and enjoy. **Don't scrutinize, don't be critical, don't be a curmudgeon, just allow yourself to capture each moment with joy and a smile.**

Funny Stories and Messages

Before I get accused of being a spoiled kid from Long Island who never learned to do his own laundry, first know that I received a practical and thoughtful gift from my grandmother to pay for a pickup and delivery laundry service while I attended college. And I also have absolutely no clue how to do my own laundry . . .

This laundry service, Good News Laundry in Evanston, Illinois, quickly became an integral part of my college experience. It was mightily convenient, noticeably consistent, and always delivered my clothes with the freshest of laundry smells. Above all, what this laundry service had and has is a fascinating owner named Kelly. Kelly and I have grown extremely close through our laundry connection. He became aware of my finest moments, when I'd give him suits for dry cleaning or pants to be hemmed. He also saw me at some of my worst moments when I'd throw in vomit stained shirts or pee covered sheets, but hey, it was college.

Kelly cared about every single person for whom he did laundry. Everybody knew when it was laundry day because Kelly would send a good morning text (I have no idea when this man ever sleeps) that demonstrated his belief in human nature and his desire for his clients to live full, worthwhile lives. Here is just a sample of his playful yet uplifting messages:

"Today is a day that hopes and dreams will prevail . . . believe. Pickups today from 6:30 to 7:30 be sure to text me :-). Thanks p.s. group texting you know who requesting payment!"

"Wow! This is what it's all about, SUMMER TIME in the makings. Nice and warmmmmmmm. Ok but one more exam/paper to perform. Don't lose sight of tomorrow's events. Laundry before to forget to set out by 6:30. 7:30 I wish to be elsewhere also :-)"

"Oh well as we now know . . . it's raining AGAIN! But that greener grass will look good this WEEKENDDDDDD :-) looking forward to your bag and that note of, "to be or not to be". 6:30-7:30pm. Stay aware and safe . . ."

The message here is not to go out in the morning and get yourself a laundry person who sends heartwarming, funny, sometimes thought provoking messages (although if you live in Evanston and need one, Kelly is your guy!). Rather, I want to encourage you to send these kinds of messages to other people or have a "funny buddy" send them to you. Accountability partners are exceptional resources and necessary for your Getting COMFY journey. Find somebody to go through this process with you, and send each other comical notes or inspiring daily messages right when you get up.

Sending these messages to other people does two things. One, you get your mind moving in that optimistic, light-hearted direction. Two, you are brightening somebody else's morning! You should not be the only person to reap the benefits of this awesomeness, so feel free to share it and involve others, all with that overall goal of bettering yourself.

Another tactic is to take time to write down and keep a collection of funny stories. I do this in the morning and throughout the rest of my day. Any hilarious situation that I encounter, I write it down and keep it in a funny folder in my notebook, or on my phone. Not only is it fun to write, but also if I am ever not feeling 100%, I can look into my funny folder to perk up, reminisce in unbelievably great moments, and release my mind from whatever tension it was that was creating that uneasiness.

Why are you happy all the time and love hugs?

"When you hug someone, you hug with the heart." "It's 1,000 words. A hug means 1,000 words." "It's like saying I'm giving you all of my love." "People love me because I'm just a person with lots of love." "My best motto is laughter is the best medicine." "Look away the negative and keep the positive." "Look at yourself in the mirror. Take a think about it. And then there's a (SNAP). That click. Oh, that makes me happy." "Find the things that you love, the passions, your desires, your hopes and dreams." "I'm happy because I'm happy of who I am." "I'm happy of being able to do whatever I want to do, be wherever I want to be." "I'm happy all the time because I love myself." "Because you got to love yourself before you love anyone else."

Take a second to guess who may have expressed these ideas. I'll give you a hint: They are magnificent people. Are they billionaires? Nope. World-renowned happiness psychologists? Nope. They are the wonderful people featured on ABC iView's "You Can't Ask That", and they all have Down syndrome. They have such a refreshing view on life that is so genuine and should force us all to take a moment and have a sense of perspective. They know exactly what makes them happy, and clearly they are not afraid to express it. More importantly, they are proud of it.

When I was in elementary school, there was a boy named Randy. I remember what made Randy's eyes light up. He started to chuckle, cry with joy, just at the sight of a lollipop. I don't know what it was, but I wanted to see Randy like that all the time, so I decided to bring Randy a lollipop every day. Each time I'd give it to him, the excitement was unmatched. It was as if every single lollipop was the first lollipop he had ever had.

That is the excitement we need to bring to all of our experiences. Randy knew exactly what made him happy, just as these people with Down syndrome know exactly what makes them happy. Leadership speaker Drew Dudley gives a spectacular TED talk in which he describes lollipop moments, and creating these instances of extreme joy for other people. Little did I know I was creating lollipop moments far before I even heard of Drew Dudley. So go out and create these moments. Do them for yourself and do them for others. Find exactly what makes you happy, and who makes you happy. Laugh at it, hug it, smile about it, and embrace it every single day.

I've never really worried about what I'm doing,
I worry more about how I'm doing it.
Tariq Farid, CEO Edible Arrangements

Y - YOU

I've gone long enough without giving appropriate credit to the hardest working, most positive, most altruistic people I know, and the main inspiration for all that I do, my parents. These are the type of people that live for their children. My brother and I are their true passions, their true interests. We are what they would focus on in the Y part of Getting COMFY, which is all about YOU. Whatever you want to do, whatever you are passionate about, spend time on it each day in the final part of your morning routine.

Every morning before he left for work at 6:30, my dad would come in to our rooms, and give my brother and me a kiss on the head before leaving. Maybe he thought we were sleeping, but we always noticed. Shortly thereafter, my mom would come walking up the steps, hands completely full having just made two breakfasts, set up little picnics on the floors of our rooms, and wake us up to the smell of whatever breakfast we asked for the night before. This was the end of my mom and dad's COMFY routines, the "you" or "your choice" for them was to put all of their energy into giving their children the best lives possible, and that they have. And not to mention, my mom made this trek every single morning battling Multiple Sclerosis. Talk about somebody who overcomes the odds to focus on the people she loves.

My brother and I mean so much to my mom that she may get a little teeny weenie bit emotional at times. In the summer of the early 2000's my brother and I were in this Ping-Pong phase, and all we wanted to do was enter tournaments and go to friends' houses to play. But we did not have a table for ourselves. After camp one day, we came home to our mom bawling. As she fought through the tears, as she often does because that is her personality, we were able to make out something related to "not here" "surprise" and "Ping-Pong table", and that was all we needed. What happened was, our parents had ordered us a Ping-Pong table and it was supposed to be set up for us by the time we got back from camp. It was going to be this great surprise, but the table never showed.

At the time and still to this day we all laugh about it because those are the people that we are. But although she may not know this, I know why she was crying. All she wanted to do was create something memorable for the people she cared about most, and it was tarnished by something that was out of her control. But that is why we were able to get over it so quickly, get her over it so quickly, and laugh about it. You cannot dwell on what is not in your control. It is a waste of mental space to be thinking what you could have done differently to influence situations in which you had no part.

My mom's passion is her kids, and that is whom she focuses on in the morning and all throughout the day. She gives to us all she possibly can without ever expecting anything in return. Because of her, I have made this my life philosophy —

Add value to as many people as possible without ever requiring or expecting anything in return.

Relinquishing self-interest is like the principle of compounding stocks. With compounding investment in stocks, the earlier you start and longer you do it, the more return you will see in the end due to interest, no matter the volatility of the market. The earlier you focus on becoming passionate and interested in adding positive value for others, the better off it will be for them and for you in the future, no matter what happens in between.

I can count on one hand the number of fights, including with my parents, that I have had in my life. But one of those fights I remember vividly. The gist is that my brother and I were being accused of only being nice when we wanted something. This is an argument that is familiar to parents and children everywhere. But hearing my mom scathingly say, "You only like us when you're asking us for something" plays in my head whenever I am interacting with anybody. I make it my duty to erase that phrase from my vocabulary, to be nice to everybody all the time, focus on her or his needs, desires, and issues. Always start conversations by asking about other people, and never make them feel like they are being used or overlooked.

One of my favorite CVS employees is a guy named Mario. Mario always has a few extra minutes to chat. He is always poking fun at my majority alcoholic purchases, and always has a smile on. I once heard him pick up the phone and immedi-

ately answer with, "Hi this is Mario. How can I make it easier?" I loved this opening line. Who will not be enticed, will not be pleased to hear somebody on the other end of the phone whose one goal is to make things easier for you? This is the way we should approach interactions with everyone we encounter.

I'm not saying do not accept anything in return if offered. If somebody on the other end of the phone awarded Mario or me $100, we would probably take it. If you are being offered a favor or any sort of compensation then obviously yes, receive it warmly, kindly, and with tremendous gratitude. What I am saying is approach people, scenarios, companies, thinking about how you can give the other party the most desirable outcome. Do not minimize your effort because of what you are getting in return, and do not hide or conceal information to spite or illustrate that you should be getting back something more favorable.

Making things easier and discovering simplicity should be one of our primary overarching ambitions. This is what the best inventions do, the best companies do, and the best people do. How often do we hear the phrases, "Life is tough" or "Life isn't fair, get used to it", when something isn't going our way? We should really get rid of that phrase and start saying the opposite. The more we hear that life can be easy, life can be fair, things have a way of working out, the more we will start to believe it and think like that as a whole.

Choosing Your Passion

Feel young, think old. One more time: feel young, think old. When I was waking up for that championship soccer game so long ago, that was the feeling I always want to have when I get up, and that is the feeling you have when you are truly infatuated by something in your life. It's the kind of feeling that has you energized, has you acting maybe a little weird, a little giddy, and has you feeling exactly how you felt when you were a child. When something in your life makes you feel and act this way, makes you light up, makes you nerd out about it, makes you forget everything else in your life even if only for a second, that is when you know you have passion.

Thinking old is about overcoming the social anxiety and social pressures associated with pursuing a passion that may seem out of the ordinary or "weird". Once you have found that special something that can make you sing and dance like you were young, you have to have an older, more mature mindset when you decide to go ahead and pursue it. Think about when you speak to your grandparents, how open, honest, and wise they seem. They'll tell you anything, reveal anything, share too much even that your parents may object and stop them mid sentence. THEY DO NOT CARE what other people think of them. They have been around the block far more times than we have, and they understand that it is pointless to not pursue something you love due to the fear of what other people may think about it.

Do something that excites you, be weird about it, be enthusiastic about it, and don't be afraid to share it with others. Realize that what others may express as weird is actually a testament to your audacity, and a reflection of their insecurity and jealousy that you have found something that you love and they have not. **There is nothing memorable about the unremarkable.**

ABCD. No, we're not talking about the alphabet. ABCD here stands for Asset Based Community Development. As a community organizer, Jody Kretzmann has been working on this concept for over four decades, and the goal is to rebuild neighborhoods by focusing on the assets and resources that the citizens *do* have rather than on what they do not have. In an impoverished community that wants to turn an abandoned lot into a garden, they will discover the capacities they have on hand, like if anybody has contracting experience, construction experience, etc. They will not look to find external parties to come in and do the work for them. It is cost minimizing, and community engagement maximizing.

This is one of the two methods for unleashing your passion. Grow and develop what you already have, what you already excel at, what comes naturally to you. You can uncover and create so much with what you already possess.

When Bruce Graham and Fazlur Khan sat down at a coffee shop to discuss changing the American architecture game, they used cigarettes to create a multi-layered structure. This cigarette structure turned into America's tallest building, The Sears Tower. You hear stories all the time, like Southwest Airlines starting on a napkin, The Gettysburg address on the back of an envelope, of remarkable accomplishments coming from the most unlikely of origins. Be resourceful and be creative anywhere. Use existing skills and whatever is available to you, and polish them every single day to engrain in your mind that you are talented, you are gifted, and you are successful.

The other method is working on something that you love, but have never tried. Something that whenever you see it, read about it, or talk about it, you're dialed in, your heart races, your eyes widen, and you cannot stop smiling. Give it a go, work on it in the morning.

Both of these methods require practice, but with something new and unnatural, repetition is the quickest way to expertise. But it is not just mindless repetition. It's the kind of repetition that becomes so painstakingly rooted into your mind and body, that even in times of despair, it is still second nature. It's what author Angela Duckworth describes as grit—a combination of perseverance and passion that is her number one factor in determining success. Work harder than you did the day before, compete against yourself, emphasize the things you can control, and the results will follow.

Paul Corona wrote a book called *The Wisdom of Walk-Ons: 7 Winning Strategies For College, Business and Life*. He outlines the walk-on mindset in which these student athletes had to work harder and smarter than everybody else on the field and in the classroom. They needed to demonstrate patience and true grit in order to get their chance, and for each of them, when that opportunity arose, they made the most of it. They turned a habit into a work ethic, and a work ethic into a passion. And that passion led to happiness.

It is said to take four weeks to turn something into a habit. Expand that habit into a passion, work on it every single day as the last part of your Getting COMFY routine, and who knows, maybe you will create the next affordable airline or world's tallest building! And when you are able to feel the emotions mentioned that are expressed for a true passion with your Getting COMFY routine, that is when you know it is right for you. That is when you have discovered the best way for you to Get COMFY.

Passion Projects

The Running Man

You're running along the shoulder, exactly as you have done every single day for the last 10 years. The classical music of NPR is playing, and the birds are chirping, creating a harmonious duet that only you have the pleasure of hearing. You make a prayer for friends and family as you pass the house on the corner with the statue outside. Your mind is relaxed. It's so peaceful. AND THEN

BOOM! A CAR COMES VEERING OFF THE SIDE OF THE ROAD AND KNOCKS YOU OFF YOUR FEET! Calm turns to calamity and what kinds of thoughts are possibly running through your head?

For Jim Fagan, his immediate concern was, "What and how do I tell my wife Sue?" That's the kind of guy Jim is, a man of faith, a man of empathy, a man who puts others, especially his wife, before himself. He is composed in situations in which others may panic. He demonstrates the Getting COMFY mindset. Thankfully for Jim, that car accident only left him with a fractured hip, it only sidelined him from one day of work, and he was back to teaching and sharing his wisdom with students the following Sunday. Within 4 months, he was on that same road, on the same shoulder, listening to the birds and the beats of NPR radio. Jim says he was lucky, but I believe it was his resilience, his faith in others, and his faith in himself that literally got him back on his feet so quickly and running again in just a few months.

Jim Fagan is an attorney and theologian by day, and a runner by morning or night. For the last 15 years, he has been looping around his Dix Hills, Long Island neighborhood for almost 2 hours each day. I had never met Jim before this conversation, but I have seen him in snow, rain, burning hot and below 0 degree weather. Allured by a pair of knee braces in CVS and the opportunity to run a half marathon with Sue and her brother, at the age of 40 Jim began to run and was the only one in that trio to complete the 13 mile race.

"I'm passionate about my wife, but running isn't necessarily a passion!" Jim mentioned to me. "It's enjoyment, it's stress-free, it's a relaxing time, time to reflect, time to pray for at least 3 people I know. I still think about other things sometimes, and work pops into my head. Thoughts come in, but it's still relaxing." But I would disagree with Jim. A passion is explored because it puts us in a state of nirvana. We become the person that we truly want to be when we are pursuing our passion. When Jim is running, he is peaceful, his thoughts are clear, he is thinking about his wife, praying for his friends. Sure, thoughts pop in from time to time, but that is what happens when your mind is free. Thoughts come and go, but the euphoria remains for that entire hour thirty, hour forty-five that Jim is outside. And think about the paradox of Jim's accident. Doing what he loved caused physical pain and agony. But the desire to get back to doing what he loved, even though it caused this distress, motivated him to get back out there. That is a passion.

Jim believes in guardian angels. On the weekends, he likes to get out at around 5 or 6 am, usually when it is still dark out, so he wears a bright vest to ensure there are no more accidents. 3 years ago on a Saturday at dawn, a car stopped him and the woman inside approached. This wasn't the most unusual of circumstances as people often stopped Jim in admiration. My mom even stopped him the other day to talk to him and set up our discussion! This lady in her thirties looked at Jim and told him that she still couldn't see the vest that well. In one swift motion, she reached into her car and said, "So I got you this new one!" Jim was awe struck. He tried to pay her for it, but all she cared about was his safety. She drove away and although he has never seen her again, Jim still wears that same vest every morning 3 years later.

Jim's daily jog has led to opportunities like the encounter with this woman. He has found guardian angels, been put through times of adversity and relentlessly fought back. Jim is the ideal candidate to show that focusing on others will eventually come back to help you in one form or another. So keep praying, keep focusing on your wife and your friends, and of course, keep on *looping around those streets, just as you do every single day.*

The Chick and the Pea

"Avete un minuto per preparare una presentazione di tre minuti sul significato dell'entusiasmo. Nessun telefono! Silenzio! Partire!" "How is that even remotely possible?" Diana thought, whose Italian was sufficient enough at the time to know this meant she had to give a presentation on the meaning of the word enthusiasm for 3 minutes, while only preparing for 1. "I was literally getting hazed by Italians. They were expressionless. No smiles. I completely blacked out during my presentation, I have no idea what I said, but I made it through it." What was supposed to be this magical study abroad experience in a remote part of Italy very quickly turned to a rigidly structured program, in which students were actually crying because they could not come up with 3 minutes of Italian explanations for enthusiasm. Anticipation became despair and optimism reversed to defeat.

This feeling was not totally new to Diana however. Maybe she had never been screamed at in a foreign language until on the verge of tears, but that feeling of navigating unfamiliar territory she knew had happened before. Diana Klonaris is from Cleveland, Ohio. She attended the same school from Kindergarten to 12th grade, and then like her older sister, decided to move away from home for college. She attended Purdue University in Indiana to study Marketing and Management, but soon after arriving, she experienced her first sign of uneasiness in regards to being uncomfortable in a new situation. "It was September, and I was ready to leave. I packed up my stuff and went home." She was fully ready to transfer, but luckily for Diana, she has some phenomenal parents, and they knew she could persevere and give Purdue another shot. She repacked her things and never looked back. She had gotten through her first feeling of defeat. She had tasted what it was like to overcome. She had Gotten COMFY.

In both scenarios, Diana arrived in an obscure location, and was immediately challenged by her environment. Her interactions and sentiments toward Purdue got better and better over time, as did her Italian. That natural feeling of trepidation faded because quite simply, Diana never gives up. That is just how she was raised. These wild, overwhelming times are the ones that are most memorable. They're the ones that are remarkable.

But surprisingly this story is not about Diana's appetite to push through seemingly impossible circumstances at school or with the Italian language. It's about a different appetite. This story is about a chick and a pea, and her hummus passion and business, The Chick and the Pea. Diana and her family live a healthy lifestyle. They like to know what is going into their bodies before they eat something, as we all should. A few years ago, Diana's mom sent her an article about Sabra Hummus and all of the hidden ingredients that were mixed into store bought hummus. It was then that Diana pledged to never eat store bought hummus again. So she started making her own.

What began as a sort of rebellion against the dangers of big hummus corporations soon developed into a hobby, and a process that was straight up fun. She'd make it with her roommate, with her mom, and all her friends would try it. She'd experiment with new flavors some of which worked, and some not so much. "Avocado and hummus are two separate flavors and they should stay that way!" Diana told me as she lit up reminiscing about the early stages of her hummus-making voyage. Most importantly though, people were making sure she knew that her hummus was really, really good, and that she had to share this talent with others. "My dad and his friends don't like hummus, they don't know anything about it. But one of his friends has told me that he can and has sat on the couch and eaten an entire container!" It's stories like that that allow Diana to fall in love with what she does.

Fast-forward to summer 2016, and Diana has commenced a new journey in the city of Chicago. Another unexplored territory, but at this point, settling and acclimating to new scenarios was a breeze. With family in the area, she was invited to a summer cookout and gathering at her cousin's house that contained an annually themed cooking competition. And guess what the theme happened to be the exact year Diana moved to Chicago? That's right, hummus. As a person who usually does not wait to seek opportunity and normally just goes for it, this was a case in which opportunity found her. The stars had aligned for Diana rather than her having to configure them herself. She had to enter.

This competition got fierce. One cousin always took the crown, but another cousin wanted to turn the tide. She called Diana to let her know that she had been practicing for weeks, and she knew that the blend she created had the right flavor profile to take this years' trophy. Diana had not made her hummus in months, so given the intensity of the competition, she decided to experiment with new ingredients a few days prior, and think about how she could differentiate herself from her cousins. After a blind taste testing, Diana's unique yet perfect combination, her red pepper and feta hummus was victorious. "I don't think I'll be invited back!" But as long as she brings this fantastic "chickpeace" offering, I'm sure they'll be happy to have her.

Product, check. Proof of concept, check. Willingness to continue, check. Now Diana had to figure out more of the logistics. She utilized her resources, people she knew, and items she had at her disposal to get in touch with designers, artists, packagers, lawyers, and even homemade salsa company owners! Talking to these people gave her the green light she needed to turn this into the real deal. But for every 10 steps she took forward, she took 5 steps back.

Regulations are aplenty when dealing with a food product and in order to get into certain farmer's markets, Diana had to cook in the right environ-ment and have the right sanitation expertise to do so. She'd fill out application after application with little feedback. One promising lead was with a woman at the Chicago farmer's market who abruptly stopped responding. But Diana is persistent, as we know. She worked her way to another contact within the same market, only to find that the original woman was out on maternity leave and she'd have to adhere to more regulations if she wanted to be in the Chicago farmer's market.

That feeling of defeat was starting to creep up on her, but this time it was different. Hummus is her passion. Not only the food itself, but also the entire process; from filling out these applications, talking to the vendors, learning about what exactly she needs to move on, to physically cooking for 7 hours in a kitchen with her mom. It's enjoyable, it's stress-free, and it's not rushed. That salsa company owner told Diana that there was no one path to building her business, and that she was going to make mistakes. Diana is embracing this idea, taking it one step at a time, focusing on the little things, and it seems to be working.

Just recently, Diana enjoyed her first farmer's market in Cleveland. I almost said "worked" her first farmer's market, but I would have been lying to you. This is not work for Diana, and this is how we should view all of our passions. This is enjoyment, it's entertainment, and this is what she reads about, posts about, smiles about. This is a *time for her to reflect, absorb, and create as much value for herself and others as possible, and that is exactly what she is doing.*

Diana is focusing on the positives from her first selling experience—the customer interaction, telling her story, visualizing in real time people's reactions as they dug into The Chick and the Pea containers. She's continuing to experiment with new varieties and hopes to have a tasting party for hungry friends and customers. Even with daunting times moving to a new state, to a new country, starting a new business, Diana has found a way to succeed. She loves giving advice and positive reassurance to anybody who is experiencing similar anxiety to what she had, because she knows that offering positive reassurance is enormous in conquering difficult scenarios. So be on the lookout for The Chick and the Pea, understand from Diana's situation how important it is to Get COMFY in un-COMFY environments, and Diana, keep selling, keep marketing, and keep kicking "humass."

The Superwoman

Aside from writing this book, or cooking as my Y, I engage in a variety of projects that I work on depending on the day. I am somebody who is more afraid of the "what could be" in not pursuing something, rather than being afraid of going out and doing it. Allow that fear of the "what if" to be stronger than the fear of doing. This will force you to really get after things that you have always wanted to try, rather than have these ideas sit in your head every night.

It is imperative to find what motivates you. Why do you do what you do? Thought leader Simon Sinek describes this as "finding your why." It is up to you to create your life mission, and you will only do so by spending time on growing and developing yourself through this routine.

Some people want to make a million dollars, other people want to make a million friends. My dream is to add value to a million people, and I don't want or expect anything in return. This is my motivation. Your motivations do not have to be complex or verbose. The why behind my motivation is quite simple—I do what I do for my parents. I already have the best parents imaginable, and I also want to make them the proudest parents imaginable.

My mom has MS, and you may be able to notice it from her slight waddle or diagonal walking, but you'd never know it from her mentality, day-to-day activity, or because she is going to tell you about it. She has sacrificed a lot since her first child was born over 27 years ago and has put all of her time and effort into raising us. Because of this, my passion project is dedicated to my mom.

Like Diana, it is another food product that was too good for solely my family and friends to be enjoying. I wouldn't say that my family has a ton of traditions, but one family staple is mandels—a cookie coming from the Jewish dessert Mandelbrot, that is like a rectangular chocolate chip biscotti. As you now know, I wasn't the leanest kid growing up and neither was my brother, so what we wanted from these mandels was more chocolate, less nuts, and a softer texture so we could take down more in one sitting. My mom has perfected this secret family recipe, catering exactly to how my brother and I liked them, to no surprise, and has baked hundreds of batches of these little "chocolate chip cookie heaven sticks" as friends like to call them.

It finally clicked for me that this was an opportunity to show my mom how much I appreciated her, and provide her with a revamped career opportunity, a passion project of her own, one that we can have fun with and work on together.

Why not start selling these mandels? Well for one, unless you're Jewish, you probably have no idea what a mandel or what Mandelbrot is, and two, why would somebody buy this cookie as opposed to others, especially in the midst of a health craze sweeping the nation?

To address the awareness for mandels dilemma, I thought, "let's advertise them as a rectangular cookie." But that is not enough. There needed to be more, and I needed to further differentiate and make people feel okay about buying a high calorie snack. People don't care what they buy, they care why they buy it.

I'm somebody who tries to give back when I can. I've worked in soup kitchens, helped Alzheimer's patients, mentored impoverished youth, and I have always been fascinated by TOMS Shoes, and how Blake Mycoskie has ignited this philanthropic capitalist movement in which companies share their profits with a charitable cause or organization. TOMS uses a one for one model in which every pair of shoes sold, one pair goes to a person in need.

I'm selling mandels for my mom, so what better way to give back to her and all of society than by creating a profit-share with the MS Society. And it hit me that I didn't need to say these were mandels, but these were MomdelS, with the M and the S capitalized so it is apparent in the logo and the spelling of the name that in buying MomdelS, you are supporting my mom and all the other moms out there, and you are also supporting MS.

Still in its early stages, I want MomdelS to stand out. Besides the fact that they are freaking delicious, in addition to the profit share I want my audience to buy MomdelS for a reason that for everyone, hits closer to home. Home, that is exactly it. Home is where the mom is, and moms make you feel warm, they make you feel safe, they make you feel happy, they make you feel COMFY. These treats aim to generate a sense of nostalgia, bringing you back to a time when you enjoyed freshly baked cookies, bringing you back to your childhood, bringing you back to a place of comfort. I envision that the packaging will be a mini house to illustrate stability in this hectic world. It will bring you back to that kid again feeling we have talked about, and will inspire you to follow whatever it was you wanted to do with your life.

MomdelS are truly the perfect complement to the Getting COMFY mindset. They represent simplicity, safety, and ease of mind. They represent *family. Your family is what you love, your friends become your family, your coworkers become your family, you never want to give up on what you love, so you never want to give up an indulgence like this. But what about the health enthusiasts, the naysayers, people even like myself, who practice health conscious eating habits? They may turn people off because they are not gluten-free, dairy-free, fat-free, whatever-free you want them to be. But even as a personal trainer, I still have one every single day. They serve as a reminder that we must cherish our lives, our opportunities, our families, and this astonishing world in which we live. Indulgences are necessary even for people dieting, because you never want to fully rid yourself of what makes you happy.*

MomdelS in moderation, a few bites to keep you optimistic about all situations, motivated about your ambitions, grateful for your childhood and your family, and COMFY with your life. **It is ultimately healthier for you to carefully invite indulgences into your life rather than neglect them.**

Allow your passion project to be anything. My dad has jokingly, but meaningfully said, "If you want to be a ditch digger, then be a dig ditcher, but make sure you dig some damn good ditches!" It does not matter what you do, what matters is how you do it. Whether they are dirty jobs, odd jobs, not jobs at all, do it because it makes you happy, because you think you are going to get something out of it, and because it is a worthwhile last thing to do in your morning before you are fully ready to Get COMFY with the rest of your day.

I don't like looking back. I'm always constantly looking forward. I'm not the one to sort of sit and cry over spilt milk. I'm too busy looking for the next cow.
Gordon Ramsay

WHAT NOW

And a rock step, triple step, triple step. And a rock step triple step, triple step. And a rock step triple step, triple step, and a lift or a dip or a jump! This is a melody I will never forget. It's the pattern and tune I learned when I took a swing dancing class, something I'd never thought I would do in my life. But I spent 10 weeks practicing it, learning the moves, maintaining constant eye contact with my partner, smiling, and putting on a final two-minute performance for over thirty people. I also have that performance on video in case anybody would ever like to see it, email me and I will gladly send it over.

I'm now 23 years old and have received my Bachelor's and Master's degrees from Northwestern University and then Kellogg School of Management. I have spent the last year testing out this COMFY mindset and putting myself in uncomfortable positions. Getting COMFY is a push to get you out of your COMFY zone, and that is exactly why I took swing dancing. It was an experience that I dreaded, that I thought I would hate, that I never thought I would excel at. But these are the experiences that are most memorable. When you Get COMFY being outside your COMFY zone, and especially when you thrive in those environments, you have positive feelings of achievement associated with these times, and these are the things you will remember most. Put yourself in foreign situations, ones in which you have to adapt. Sign up for a random class, go to a networking event in a field in which you have no background, experience a life outside of your common ground.

What's best to do now, if you have not already, is to start trying out new things in the morning, waking up earlier and working on yourself. Calm your mind and your body by stretching or practicing meditation. Open up and allow yourself to be vulnerable with yourself and with others. Move around your room or your neighborhood. Laugh or smile at something funny to give yourself perspective and take your day a little less seriously. And then focus on you, so that you can become the person you want to spend all of your time with. If you're somebody who feels better with a definitive sample routine, here it is below! Remember to first set that alarm and then immediately put those feet on the floor!

C – Get the mind calm, meditate

O – Start smiling. Write in your gratefulness journal

M – Get the body charged, do jumping jacks

F – Laugh. Watch a video or read a funny meme

Y – Get ready for the day, practice your passion

What I have not provided in these sections is set timing for each activity. I have not done so because it is up to you to feel out what gets you the most in tune with your routine. These are recommendations, not demands, and the more freedom you have in deciding your own morning, the more personalized it becomes, and the more excited you will be to wake up and immediately practice something that is yours.

What I have provided throughout these sections are bolded phrases that I believe are the most important mottos or lessons to be taken from Getting COMFY, and applied to our entire lives. These are not the implementable IDUHS that you should immediately start including in your life, but rather, these are the ideas to look at when wondering why or how to get through difficult situations and keep on Getting COMFY. Instead of having you scour through the book to find them, I have provided them below. Read through and have them act as the motivation to start and continue Getting COMFY.

15 Reminders to Keep Getting COMFY

1. **Together, we are going to Get COMFY waking up in the morning, Get COMFY in un-COMFY situations, Get COMFY in our own skin, and Get COMFY with the way we live the rest of our lives.**

2. **The more you invest in yourself, the more able you are to help those around you and succeed in what you really desire.**

3. A major part of enjoying every morning is to reach inside for the kid in you and not be afraid to outwardly portray your excitement for the day ahead.

4. Go to bed smiling, wake up happy.

5. We spend more time with ourselves than anybody else in the world. So why not work on, polish, and Get COMFY with the person with whom we spend so much time?

6. Being vulnerable, asking for help, acknowledging weakness, should never be misconstrued as something to hide or as a sign of defeat. We must go about life asking questions, becoming curious, incessantly searching to learn and discover as much as we possibly can.

7. Be able to receive help just as easily and as well as you can provide it.

8. Overcoming the fear of failure, the fear of mistakes, the fear of embarrassment, the fear of losing, and expressing vulnerability in a way

that is justifiable are the most crucial aspects of self-expression and the primary factors in living life stress-free.

9. Fully entrench yourself with thoughts and actions that are most meaningful and beneficial to you, and all the stress, trouble, and worry will disappear. And even if it is just for a moment, and the worries come back, you are now realizing that they are possible to overcome.

10. Finding time to laugh, or more importantly just finding time to smile in any circumstance completely adjusts your mindset, and provides a greater opportunity to better cope with any situation.

11. Smile until your face starts to hurt.

12. Don't scrutinize, don't be critical, don't be a curmudgeon, just allow yourself to capture each moment with joy and a smile.

13. **Add value to as many people as possible without ever requiring or expecting anything in return.**

14. **There is nothing memorable about the unremarkable.**

15. **It is ultimately healthier for you to carefully invite indulgences into your life rather than neglect them.**

There you have it. Your foolproof guide to more enjoyable mornings and more productive, worthwhile days. Your Morning Guide to Daily Happiness. But wait, one last thing . . .

The Kicker

It's a great day to be a great day. A line so often used by my group of friends, but not often used enough by the rest of the world. It takes one look around your room, one look at your surroundings, one look outside to realize this marvelous wonder we call life. So wake up just a little earlier, smile just a little wider, and in the wise words of Randall from *This Is Us*, "Take a walk. Slow it down a little. Talk to the mailman." Because at the end of the day all we are able to influence are things that we can control.

Things like the pace of our life, the actions we choose, the conversations we have, and the people with which we surround ourselves. Our ability to proceed to the future and our inability to time travel back to the past are our greatest gifts.

That's what this is really all about—understanding, analyzing, getting comfortable with, and responding to any situation. Moving on to the next one, not dwelling on the past, and improving no matter the consequence. Because at the end of the day once things happen, you **C**an **O**nly **M**ove **F**orward, **Y**es?

COMFY

ACKNOWLEDGEMENTS

I just read a few different acknowledgements pages from some of my favorite books, and I want to start in a way I have not seen. There I go again, always trying to reinvent the wheel. But I think this time it's worth it.

My first and foremost token of gratitude is for YOU, the reader. The friend, the stranger, the parent, the daughter, the son, the grandparent, the athlete, the computer wiz, the outcast, the introvert, the extrovert, the fan, whoever it is that is reading this, I thank you. I hope that this guide adds as much value to your life as you all have added to mine.

Getting COMFY is the result of a once in a blue moon project that turned into a full-fledged effort to inspire millions. This morning practice has become so much more than a 30-minute start to my day. It has become my release, my celebration, my topic of conversation, my identity, and I plan for it to continue just like this as more and more people are inspired and come aboard onto the movement. But I could not have done this without support obviously. There are so many people I am grateful for who have been a part of this process. Unfortunately I can't name everyone individually, but I have to mention a couple.

Mom, Dad, and Adam. This is it. I could end the acknowledgements right here because you are the reasons I do what I do. A family of four turned to four best friends as Adam and I grew older, all I wish to accomplish, all I wish to experience, all I wish to instill in others, I do for you guys. Thank you for being my support, my motivation, and my biggest fans.

To Grandma Harriet and Grandma Elly, the little young ladies who bring me so much laughter and joy. I hope I do the same for you. Thank you for being the only people in the world who will not care to even mention a word about themselves, and focus the entire conversation on me every time we speak. Love you both so much, and I know I have to come to Queens a little bit more often!

Grandpa Morty and Grandpa David. I think about you guys everyday. It's been years since you passed, but I think you'd be pretty proud of the man I've become. I've combined the wit and playfulness of Grandpa Morty with the wisdom, patience, and genuine kindness of Grandpa David to become a distant second to the superhuman you two combined made.

I was always told how difficult it was going to be to stay close to my home friends after high school. But after over 5 years of different counties, countries, and continents, I think we could write the playbook on how to remain best friends. The laughs and smiles are endless, and the relationships we've been able to maintain for such a long time are truly unmatchable.

I was also told how incredible the relationships I was going to make with my college friends were going to be. I couldn't fathom at the time how this could be true, but after 4 years at Northwestern and 1 at Kellogg, I could not have dreamt up a better group of people. After traveling the world with you all, living with you all, spending every single day and night at your houses or apartments, I have realized the tremendous value you have added to my life, and I hope I have and can continue to do the same for you moving forward.

There is also a very special group of people who have done work by both appearing in and assisting with the writing and editing process along the way. None of this would have come out the way it did without all of your help, feedback, and guidance.

Jake, our relationship is one that doesn't even need an acknowledgement like this. But your commitment, contribution, and courage to appear in and support the *Getting COMFY* movement, and to support me, is something that far surpasses anything I could even draw up on paper. You're a whole different caliber of person and you drive me to just get a little bit better each day.

Marissa, I could not be more thankful for the work you did as I was writing this book, and for the lack of work you were getting at your actual job! You were there proofreading every single paragraph, and I can't thank you enough. It takes a really special person to do the research, give the feedback, and provide the recommendations you did, and I am more appreciative than you could ever imagine for all you've done for me.

To a very special group of readers who served as the best editing team, thank you so much. Adam, Ariel, Rap, Cam, Nick, Eddie, Steven, Mom, Dad, Jake, Don, Jonny – you each provided me with a different idea to build upon, a sentence to rearrange, or a typo to fix. You all caught every single thing, and I thank you so much for taking the time and effort to read beforehand and make fantastic improvements.

ACKNOWLEDGEMENTS

To my roommates and extended roommates Erik, Mikey, Jake, Don, Heyman, Robby, Derek, Arkin, Jonah, Ocko, Brodie, Nick, Huddy, Mano, Ehinger. Thank you for putting up with how much I talked about this book, for helping me choose the right cover, for making social media accounts, for connecting me with the right people, and for simply building me up rather than putting me down as I pursued this project.

A very special thanks to Marilu Henner, actress and New York Times bestselling author of 10 books, who took time out of her day to read, provide feedback, and have multiple phone calls and text conversations with me. You are an incredibly special person!

To the stars and their stories – Ross Goldberg, Austin Carr, Jake Freeman, Jeff Kelly, Diana Klonaris, and Jim Fagan – I am blown away by your stories, your willingness to help me, and your willingness to help others with the openness you displayed by appearing in *Getting COMFY*. You each bring a unique perspective that gives this work an identity that can associate with people from all walks of life. Thank you so much.

Ehinger, my very own computer wiz, thank you for being so interested in helping, and doing everything I asked with ease and a smile. It's one thing to help and go through the motions, but it's another to help and make me feel like you were excited to do so, which I cannot appreciate enough. It's an amazing quality you have, and people should feel lucky and honored to work with you.

To Ariel, my PR Rep! You have such a very special talent in this space, and I am so excited to continue working with you! You really do have a knack for this, and I can't wait for the tremendous success you are going to have!

To Chris Friesen, my accountability buddy, Canadian pen pal, whatever you want to call it, thanks for our weekly calls and for walking me through the ins and outs of the publishing process. You're a great guy, and I look forward to working with you more and more moving forward!

To the entire launch team, everybody that heard about this guide beforehand, anybody that read it, was interested in it, left a review, downloaded an eBook, told a friend about it, or just listened to me talk about it, you are the reasons this is a success. I could not do it without all of you, and I cannot explain the level of gratitude I have for spreading the word and love about the *Getting COMFY* movement.

ACKNOWLEDGEMENTS

To all of the people who have influenced me with your books, courses, podcasts, or just general existence – Tony Robbins, Hal Elrod, Tim Ferriss, Simon Sinek, Angela Duckworth, Paul Corona, Drew Dudley, Ellen DeGeneres, Oprah, among many others—you are all inspirations and I hope to become even half the person that you all are today.

And finally to SPS, the Self-Publishing School, for helping guide me through this process. Lisa Zelenak, Chandler Bolt, Scott Allan, and formatting specialist Jen Henderson, I appreciate what you guys do, and the concept behind this wonderful program. If any of you readers are ever interested in writing your own book, try this program out: https://xe172.isrefer.com/go/curcust/bookbrosinc5328

GETTING *COMFY* WITH FEEDBACK!

I am so thankful that you have taken this Getting COMFY journey alongside me, and I am more than thrilled that you have made it to the very end! I hope that this guide has made you think a little bit differently, act a little bit differently, and has inspired you to change even just one part of your life for the better. I know this process has dramatically changed mine.

I have been dishonest and I sincerely apologize for this. I told you that every part of Getting COMFY was for you and about you. While 99.9% of that is true, I do ask for one teenie weenie little favor from you.

I mentioned how important it is to be able to both provide and receive feedback for others. I am taking my own advice and allowing for you as the reader to practice giving feedback.

So, if you enjoyed *Getting COMFY: Your Morning Guide to Daily Happiness*, if you took one thing away, took 10 things away, or just want to let me know in a few words how this book made you feel...

Then please leave a review at Amazon!

Your feedback is so important and appreciated, and if you would like to contact me directly about it, please email me at Jordan@getting-comfy.com.

I look forward to hearing from you!

Jordan

ABOUT THE AUTHOR

When Jordan was 7 years old, he had a lemonade stand. He sold cookies and lemonade and water and raised over $1,000 in a day!

It says "raised" though because this was no ordinary lemonade stand. This lemonade stand was set up on September 21st, 2001, 10 days after 9/11, and all the money was donated to families in need. For as long as he can remember Jordan was always more interested in the impact money, food, water, emotional support, you name it, could make on others than it could on him.

Jordan's mindset is to add as much value to as many people as possible without expecting anything in return. He likes to build his life to become as creative a story as possible. Because of this, he's worked with a ton of different people, in a wide range of industries, on a wide variety of projects. He was co-founder and co-contributor for a food and fitness blog called Feast Mode. He was Founder of a food delivery service called Feed My Mates and a consumer product called MomdelS. He worked with various startups including Pak'd a healthy meal delivery kit for elementary/middle school lunches, Chowbus, a food delivery service delivering authentic Asian cuisine, and RXBAR, a no BS protein bar company which was just acquired by Kellogg's. He was also a top soccer goalie in New York State in High School, and competed on a team that was ranked 3rd in the country.

Currently, Jordan is working to build the Getting COMFY brand, and is expanding this to the non-profit space, with an idea called Fed Up. With this, he hopes to bridge the gap between homelessness and job opportunities in the food service industry, and introduce a unique culinary training program for at risk millennials to Get COMFY cooking and Get COMFY with their lives.

If you wish to ever get in touch with Jordan at all for speaking engagements, article quotes, podcast opportunities, or seriously just to say hi, feel free to call, text, or email him at:

jordan@getting-comfy.com or 631-223-5956

SUP

Please reach out and get in touch with me! I'll give you a few different ways to do so:

1.   Email me at Jordan@getting-comfy.com

2.   Email me at Jordan.c.gross2016@gmail.com

3.   Call, Text, FaceTime at 631-223-5956

4.   Follow us on Instagram: https://www.instagram.com/getting_comfy/

5.   Follow us on Twitter: https://twitter.com/Getting_COMFY

6.   Subscribe to the email list: http://getting-comfy.com/

7.   Read the blog: http://getting-comfy.com/blog/

This book, this community, this movement is 100% devoted to providing you with the recommendations necessary to getting a little bit better every morning and every day. Join us!

REFERENCES

"57%   Of Americans Hit the Snooze Button." *Sleep Review*, 27 Aug. 2014, www.sleepreviewmag.com/2014/08/americans-snooze-button-withings/.

"America's Finest News Source." *The Onion*, www.theonion.com/.

Amoruso, Sophia. "Girl Boss." *Girlboss Radio*, www.girlboss.com/podcast/.

Buchanan, Leigh. "Zumba Fitness: Company of the Year." *Inc.com*, Inc., 4 Dec. 2012, www.inc.com/magazine/201212/leigh-buchanan/zumba-fitness-company-of-the-year-2012.html.

Carr, Austin. "Interview With Austin Carr." May 2017.

Cat, Big, and PFT. "Pardon My Take." *Barstool Sports*, www.podcastone.com/pardon-my-take.

Corona, Paul L. *The Wisdom of Walk-Ons: 7 Winning Strategies For College, Business And Life*. CreateSpace, 2012.

DeGeneres, Ellen. *The Ellen DeGeneres Show*, NBC.

Douglas, Genevieve. "Millennials Report Higher Rates of Depression, Need Support." *Bloomberg*, 21 Feb. 2017, www.bna.com/millennials-report-higher-n57982084118/#!

Duckworth, Angela. *Grit*. Vermilion, 2017.

Dudley, Drew. "Everyday Leadership." TEDx. TEDx Toronto, 12 Jan. 2018, Toronto, Toronto, www.ted.com/talks/drew_dudley_everyday_leadership.

Elrod, Hal. "Achieve Your Goals ." *Hal Elrod International* , halelrod.com/podcast/.

Elrod, Hal. *The Miracle Morning: the Not-so-Obvious Secret Guaranteed to Transform Your Life before 8AM*. Hal Elrod International, Inc., 2016.

Ferriss, Tim. "The Tim Ferriss Show." *The Tim Ferriss Show*, tim.blog/podcast/.

Ferriss, Timothy. *The 4-Hour Workweek: Escape 9-5, Live Anywhere, and Join the New Rich.* Harmony Books, 2012.

Fogelman, Dan, et al. "This Is Us/What Now?" *This Is Us*, season 1, episode 17, NBC, 7 Mar. 2017.

Freeman, Jake. "Interview With Jake Freeman ." May 2017.

Fricke, Ron, director. *Samsara.* Oscilloscope Laboratories, 2011.

Goldberg, Ross. "Interview With Ross Goldberg." Apr. 2017.

Gross, Jordan, and Diana Klonaris. "The Chick and the Pea." 19 June 2017.

Gross, Jordan, and Jim Fagan. "The Running Man." 15 June 2017.

Hadoukentheband. "People Are Awesome." *YouTube*, YouTube, 2014, www.youtube.com/channel/UCIJolLcABPdYGp7 pRMGccAQ.

"Meditation and Mindfulness Made Simple." *Headspace*, www.headspace.com/.

Munrow100. "The New Colony Six - Things I'd Like To Say (1969) HQ." *YouTube*, YouTube, 27 Apr. 2013, www.youtube.com/watch?v=ap8VU61Q5Ok.

Paul, Kari. "Why Some CEOs Are Finally Treating Mental Health Days as Sick Days." *MarketWatch*, 15 July 2017, www.marketwatch.com/story/why-some-companies-are-treating-employee-mental-health-days-like-sick-days-2017-02-13.

"A Potted (Early) History of Asset-Based Community Development." *Nurture Development*, 20 Oct. 2016, www.nurturedevelopment.org/blog/a-potted-early-history-of-asset-based-community-development/.

Raz, Guy. "How I Built This with Guy Raz." *How I Built This*, www.npr.org/podcasts/510313/how-i-built-this.

Robbins, Tony. "Tony Robbins Podcast." *Tony Robbins Podcast*, Robbins Research International, www.tonyrobbins.com/podcasts/.

Shepherd, Jack. "21 Pictures That Will Restore Your Faith In Humanity." *BuzzFeed*, 2012, www.buzzfeed.com/expresident/pictures-that-will-restore-your-faith-in-

humanity?utm_term=.oqjZbMKjBO#.mlKqG2Lp
9X.

Sinek, Simon. *Start with Why: How Great Leaders Inspire Everyone to Take Action.* Portfolio/Penguin, 2013.

sunsetprincess57. "RONNIE RICE - 'I WILL ALWAYS THINK ABOUT YOU.'" *YouTube*, YouTube, 31 Jan. 2010, www.youtube.com/watch?v=p2AXIuMzAHA.

Suzuki, Shunryu, et al. *Zen Mind, Beginner's Mind.* Shambhala, 2011.

Wiking, Meik. *The Little Book of Hygge: Danish Secrets to Happy Living.* Thorndike Press, a Part of Gale, Cengage Learning, 2017.

"You Can't Ask That." *ABC IView*, iview.abc.net.au/programs/you-cant-ask-that/LE1617H002S00#pageloaded.

DON'T FORGET YOUR FREE BONUS GIFT!

Start Your Getting COMFY journey now
with a sample routine!

Find it here: http://getting-comfy.com/

88989474R00114

Made in the USA
Lexington, KY
21 May 2018